MW00680956

I Am Dangerous

The Moment You Decide to Follow Jesus...Anywhere

Jen Dawson

I am Dangerous
Copyright © 2012 Jen Dawson

Scriptures taken from The Holy Bible, New International Version®,
NIV® Copyright © 1973, 1978, 1984, 2011 by Biblica, Inc.™ Used
by permission. All rights reserved worldwide.
ISBN: 978-1-77069-639-6

Word Alive Press
131 Cordite Road, Winnipeg, MB R3W 1S1
www.wordalivepress.ca

Printed in Canada

Library and Archives Canada Cataloguing in Publication
Dawson, Jen, 1975-
    I am dangerous : the moment you decide to follow
Jesus-- anywhere / Jen Dawson.
    ISBN 978-1-77069-639-6
        1. Dawson, Jen, 1975-. 2. Christian biography. I. Title.
BR1725.D39A3 2012   270.092   C2012-903567-X

Dedication

Dedicated to each person mentioned in this book, as they have each played an integral role in my walk with God. Also to all my readers; may you read it and know that while I may have lived the story and written about it, I am certainly not the author.

Contents

Introduction

For as long as I can remember, I've thought about writing a book. I never got more than a page or two written, however, before I found myself at a loss for words and quit. I really do enjoy writing, and anyone who has ever sent me a four-sentence email can vouch for that, since they're likely to have received an eight-paragraph reply in return.

When I was in public school, I thought I would become a lawyer. Being a lawyer, I would be able to put my writing to good use as I wrote out my arguments. Not only that, but I really enjoy public speaking and won numerous awards for that throughout school. The thought of writing and presenting my arguments before a jury was highly appealing to me.

By the time I was in high school, I knew I wouldn't be a lawyer. I had no desire whatsoever to spend that many years studying. I decided that maybe police work was more my style. I would still be working in the legal field, but dealing more with people than stacks of paperwork.

That didn't end up happening, either. I've had all sorts of jobs over the years, in an attempt to figure out what I really wanted to do. I've worked in restaurants, grocery stores, hotels, hospitals, and banks.

After returning to school, I finally landed in the wonderful world of IT (information technology). I currently work at the computer helpdesk of a large company, and I love it. For most people, this is considered an entry-level position, and their goal is to move away from the helpdesk as quickly as possible. This is not the case for me. I love the mix of computers and people. I especially enjoy being able to help others who are stuck with a problem. I have great coworkers, a great boss (several great bosses in a row, actually), get paid well for what I do, and I'm good at my job. It has taken me many years to find such complete satisfaction with my work, but I'm very grateful to have finally achieved this.

In fact, every single area of my life is good right now. I have an incredible husband who is perfect for me in every way, I have the most amazing family and friends, I am healthier than I've ever been, and each day seems to somehow get even better than the one before.

To those reading this, you may be thinking, *Well, good for you.* You should know that it has been a long road getting here. It wasn't always easy, and to be honest, I never really imagined that the life I'm living right now would be possible. It excites me to no end to realize that it is.

A couple of months ago, a good friend of mine, Bethany, said to me over coffee, "Is there anything in life that has eluded you? Anything that you feel you've wanted to do but missed out on?"

I thought about that for a minute. "No, I don't think so. My life feels very complete. I don't think I've missed out on anything."

After a few minutes, I realized that wasn't completely true.

"Wait a minute, there is something! I've always felt as though I was going to write in some capacity. In the past few years, I've felt that I would write a book, but it just hasn't happened for me."

"What would you write about?" Bethany asked.

My answer came quickly. "My life. I've had so many crazy things happen in my life, both good and bad, that I actually find my life pretty interesting. It might be nice to share my story with others."

Bethany thought this was a great idea, so she decided to pray about this for me. She would pray that I find the time and desire to complete this one thing that had been teasing me off and on for the past few years.

I left the coffee shop thinking about this and concluded that maybe she was right. Maybe my life wasn't a hundred percent complete yet. Maybe there was still this one thing I had to do.

Of course, life gets busy and sometimes finding the time to do the things you want isn't as easy as it seems. The days went by and, while I would think of it every once in a while, I couldn't seem to think of a beginning, which prevented me from starting at all.

A couple of months later, Bethany and I visited again.

"Hey, how is that book coming?" she asked.

I admitted that I hadn't even started it yet.

"You are aware that I plan to hold you accountable, right?" she said. "I'm not going to stop asking about this until you've completed it!"

Suddenly I felt pressure—in a good way—to actually follow through.

As I drove home that night, I thought about my inability to come up with a beginning—and then it hit me: the problem was that I was trying to write *my* story. The truth is, as interesting as my life has been, it's not actually my story that I want people to read about; it's *God's* story. The God stories are what have made my life so interesting. My focus was off, which prevented me from knowing what to write. Once I realized my deep desire to share all of my God stories, the ideas flowed and this book of mine no longer became an intimidating thing, but something I could barely type quickly enough.

Some of the God stories in my life are very small, very simple, and can be shared in a paragraph or less. Some, however, are larger than life and intense. They will be a challenge to write, I'm sure, as I'll have to relive them in order to do them justice. You may or may not believe in the God of the Bible, but by the time you've finished reading about all the God stories that make up my life, I'm convinced you'll at least be able to see that this life of mine couldn't have been led by me alone. There's no possible way I would have gotten to this happy, satisfied place without some seriously divine intervention.

It is my prayer that, in reading this, you'll see me for who I am, you'll see yourself in ways you never thought possible, and you'll see God in all His glory.

This is "my" story.

The Early Years

My childhood was pretty standard, for the most part. There was lots of good, some bad, and plenty in between.

I was born and raised in Strathroy, Ontario. I have two parents who love each other and love their children. I am the youngest of three girls, and admittedly the "baby" of the family. I'm sure I was spoiled as a child, but at the time I didn't feel as though I received more or less than my sisters.

All my earliest childhood memories are good ones. I was healthy, happy, and everything in the world was good. I was happier playing with cars and trucks in the sandbox with the boys than I was playing with dolls and other girls. I was the little boy my dad never had and I loved hanging out with him. I would go play at the arena while he coached hockey, I would watch his baseball games, and he would try to give me advice on how to be a better soccer player— but one thing everyone learned about me at a very early age is that I don't accept criticism well, even if it's constructive. I am stubborn and determined, and I can figure things out on my own.

I loved my mom, but I was Daddy's little girl. My dad owned and operated the town garbage collection company and any time they passed by our school to pick up garbage while we were outside for recess, me and my friends would race over to the fence to wave and say hi. My dad was always so nice to everyone, I was proud to show him off. Sometimes he even let me ride on the step at the side of the truck. I felt famous when he let me do that.

I never knew either of my grandfathers, as they both passed away before I was born. My dad's mom passed away when I was in Grade Four and my mom's mom passed away when I was in Grade Eight. These were my first experiences with death and loss, and although they made me very sad, both my grandmothers seemed very old to me, so it seemed natural and not so devastating.

I started babysitting when I was twelve, then took over my older sister's paper route for a while before landing my first real job as a busgirl when I was just thirteen years old. I've always held a job since that time; often, I would have two jobs at once.

I wasn't a star athlete by any stretch of the imagination, but I enjoyed sports and played soccer for quite a few years. I was on a swim team for two summers, enjoyed riding my bicycle, and I have always, always loved to dance. I spent a good part of my youth in front of the basement television watching music videos on Much Music and trying to memorize the dance moves. To this day, when I'm home alone for any length of time, I crank up the music and have my own little dance party.

I got an award in Grade Six for being the "best all-around student." It was presented in front of the school and my mom even surprised me by being there when I received it. It never made me feel better than others. I actually felt a little embarrassed to receive it, but my parents were very proud of me. I was humbled.

I was careful to always remind myself that I was never better than anyone else. That comes from being picked on when I was really young. For some strange reason, there was a group of girls three or four years older than me who singled me out and made fun of me when I was in kindergarten and Grade One. They always made fun of really bizarre things, too. For example, my sisters and I are each three years apart in age. I would wait anxiously to get their hand-me-downs because I tended to love the clothes they wore. Sometimes, though, I wore clothes that were incredibly outdated. One winter when I was in Grade One, I wore a bright blue snowsuit with neon orange and yellow stripes running down the sleeves. Neon comes and goes every so many years, but by the time I was wearing it, it was long out of fashion. These girls made a point of approaching me and my friends, who were playing in a snow fort, and made fun of me for my neon snowsuit.

Oddly enough, I just found it strange that girls so much older would care about what I was wearing. My friends never seemed to care, either, so it didn't affect me. What it *did* do was make me want to be incredibly nice and kind toward others, because I never wanted to be "that girl" to the people around me. This was evident when I would walk down the hallway in Grade Seven or Eight and every little kid in school would say "Hi Jennifer!" as I walked by. I always made sure to speak to the younger kids and never missed a chance to say, "Hi! How are you?"

I first became very aware of my body image in Grade Eight when I missed two jumps during high-jump and was down to my last attempt. A male teacher said to me, "You know why you keep missing it, don't you?"

"Because I have no lift in my jump?" I asked.

"No. It's because your butt is too big."

I was so angry that I made the next jump. He thought he was brilliant in making me angry enough to complete the jump, but what he never realized was that in that very moment, he did some serious damage. I tucked that comment away in the back of my brain and it would come back in a few short years to haunt me.

The Life and Times
of a Teenager

In high school, I was neither popular nor invisible, falling some-where in the middle. I was happy with that. I had crushes on boys but never really dated anyone, and the crushes always passed. I started to become more interested in girly things like clothes and makeup and gossip—and my poor dad didn't know what to do with me. We drifted apart during my teen years, and it was during this time that I felt much closer to my mom. We talked about everything and I felt as though I could share anything with her.

When I was in Grade Eleven, my mom considered going to the Beverly Hills Weight Loss Clinic in town. It had just opened and was all the rage. I told her that maybe we could do that together and hold each other accountable. I didn't really feel as though either of us needed to lose weight, but I figured losing ten pounds couldn't hurt. She agreed, and even offered to pay for me. They measured our wrists, took our height, weighed us, and determined from that our ideal weights.

My girl told me that I was overweight by ten to fifteen pounds. Overweight? I had never viewed myself as overweight. My teach-er's comments came rushing back to me and I started to wonder if I had been in denial. Had I been overweight this whole time? I stuck to the diet plan that was laid out for me and slowly the weight came off. When I had lost about ten pounds, people started noticing and telling me how good I looked. All I could think was that I hadn't been ten pounds overweight, but ten to *fifteen* pounds. I had to get that last five off.

I stuck to the diet faithfully, but the scale wouldn't budge another pound. The girl reassured me that I had just hit a plateau and I would start to lose again in time, but a week became two and two became three and still nothing. Finally, I resorted to forcing myself to throw up to get the scale to move. The thing about doing that is that when you rid yourself of everything you've eaten, you become incredibly hungry. So I binged. It didn't really matter what I ate or how much, because I'd just lose it afterward anyway. Apparently I wasn't very good at being bulimic, though, because I would purge to the point of exhaustion and know that I hadn't gotten rid of all the junk I had eaten. Not only did I not lose weight, I gained a few pounds! It was a vicious cycle.

My weight became all I could think about. My grades dropped, my moods swung, and my innocence slipped away with every bite of food I kept track of and vowed to lose. I knew that what I was doing wasn't healthy, but I was so focused on my appearance that I didn't care.

That is, until one day my nose started to drip water for no apparent reason. I had heard that causing yourself to vomit did a lot of damage from the acid coming back up, which could ruin your teeth, damage your throat, and even hurt your nasal cavity. I wasn't too concerned about the consequences, though—just the results. My randomly runny nose scared me enough to realize that I had to stop, and quickly.

For the most part, I did quit purging, but every once in a while I had such severe food cravings that I would quiet them with an entire box of ice cream. Then I'd feel guilty and promise myself, "This is the last time." The eating disorder still had a grip on me, and my self-esteem was taking a daily hit.

One Friday night, my friends and I intended to go to a dance and my mom told me last minute that I couldn't go. There was no real reason; she just didn't think I needed to go to this dance. I pleaded with her and let her know that I had to because I had already told the other girls I could drive.

"Fine," she said. "Pick them up and drop them off at the dance, but then come home. They'll have to find their own rides home."

In the real world, missing out on a dance isn't a big deal, but in teenage-land, this was devastating. Dropping them off and seeing them all walk into the building talking and laughing while I had to turn around and go home seemed like the last straw to me. I was tired of feeling fat, tired of watching my grades continue to drop, tired of everything.

5

I pulled out of the parking lot. As I drove down the road, I realized that I was coming up to a stop sign and I would have to turn either right or left. If I went straight through the sign, I would hit a tree. I pulled the car over, undid my seatbelt, and thought that what I really wanted to do was drive as fast as I could into that tree. I don't know how long I sat there, but I do know that I couldn't get myself to do it. I sat for a long time crying, thinking that I couldn't even get my suicide right. I made my way home, went straight to bed, and wondered as I cried myself to sleep if it was humanly possible to feel any lower.

Something amazing happened when I woke up the next morning. I felt better! It occurred to me that if I had hit my lowest, then I couldn't possibly feel any worse, which meant things *had* to improve. The knowledge that there was nowhere to go but up seemed incredibly encouraging and I started to want to do better, feel better, and be better.

What finally saved me was that I applied to take part in a Rotary Student Exchange and was accepted. I spent a year living and studying in Brazil. Brazilians tend to be shorter and quite a bit thinner than their North American counterparts. I was called "fatty" on a regular basis. You'd think this would have sent me running to the nearest bathroom, but it actually did the exact opposite. One look at their narrow frames and it was easy to see that even if I weighed a hundred pounds, at five-foot-nine, I would still be wider and taller than them and they would still consider me fat. That helped me realize how ridiculous I was being. I am a very healthy weight and body shape. I'll always be thinner than some and heavier than others. I can only fairly compare myself to others who are the exact same age, height, and frame, and how often does that happen? While in Brazil, I learned to love my body for what it was—perfectly imperfect.

I returned home with a newfound confidence and the ability to read, write, and speak in another language, which reinforced in my mind that I *was* intelligent and that grades aren't always indicative of a person's mind or abilities. It's interesting, though, how confidence built on nothing substantial can be shattered so severely, and so quickly.

After being home for a week, a friend of mine invited me to a party. She said it would be a good chance to reacquaint myself with everyone before school started up again in a few weeks. I joined her, and that night I saw Ben for the first time. I thought he was cute and decided that I wanted to date him—based on that alone. Not knowing a single thing about him, I threw myself at him shamelessly and by the end of the night we were making out. We started to date immediately and things were about to change for me in a hurry.

I like to refer to Ben as my biggest mistake. I hold no ill will toward him and he actually taught me a lot. At the time, though, this was an extremely unhealthy relationship. Ben did subtle and not-so-subtle things to belittle me and make me question myself. He never took me out on dinner dates; we only had dinner together if it was free because either he was eating at my parents' place, or I was eating at his. The one time he finally said he wanted to take me out, it was because he had a coupon that said "buy one spaghetti dinner, get a second dinner free." Of course, he didn't feel like eating spaghetti that night, so…

He also did things such as pick me up to go to a party and, as I came out to the car, say something along the lines of "You're not going to wear that, are you?", making me feel incredibly self-conscious. I would go back into the house to change. These may not seem like big things, but having them happen repeatedly for two years caused me to believe I wasn't worthy of being treated to dinner or a movie, that I was only good for sex—and only when he wanted to—and that my opinion was so worthless that I couldn't even figure out how to pick an appropriate outfit to wear.

In just shy of two years, I had lost everything about me that was good and picked up everything about him that was bad. I started smoking because he did; kissing him tasted awful unless I smoked as well. I started smoking marijuana because he did and if I wanted to spend time with him, it meant being where he was and doing what he was doing. We started out moving so quickly that sleeping together just seemed like a natural progression, but there's nothing good or right about giving yourself in every way to someone who doesn't care about you in the least. I tried desperately to hold onto this unhealthy relationship, because it was too hurtful to think that I had given someone my everything and it might not be good enough.

I remember sitting in the cafeteria with some guy friends while in college talking about our significant others. I didn't really have much nice to say about my boyfriend. One of the guys asked me why I was still dating him if he wasn't even nice to me. I replied, "I've put nearly two years into this relationship. I could break up with him and find someone else, but he would likely treat me the same way and what's the point in starting over when I'm already used to what I have?" This guy looked at me as though I had just arrived from Mars. He didn't take me to task on it, but I could tell he thought that was awful reasoning. Of course, it was.

The breaking point came when I visited Ben at university one weekend. He was particularly aloof and the last time we were together, it was evident that he didn't even care to be there. He was very much going through the motions. I didn't sleep at all that night and I woke up feeling as though I had completely prostituted myself. I drove home in a daze, wondering what I had been doing with my life. How had I fallen so far? I always said that I didn't believe in breaking up with someone over the phone, because I thought it was cowardly, but the truth is that I had lost all feeling for him by the time I got home. I didn't care if he ever called me again. I didn't care if I ever saw him again. I let a week or so pass, then made up my mind to end things. I called him to say I was sorry, but we just weren't good together and I didn't think we should see each other anymore. His response was, "Oh, good. I've been meaning to break up with you for a while, but I just didn't know how."

He may have felt as though he'd lost two years of his life dating a girl who wouldn't end up being the one for him, but I felt as though I had lost my soul. I became a shell of myself and it took many years to get back to being the person I was meant to be.

One good thing that came of it was that I hung up the phone and immediately felt as though the weight of the world had been lifted off my shoulders. Within a week, I watched as my skin cleared up and nearly glowed. I swear my hair looked longer and shinier than it ever had. I quit smoking, started running longer distances, and lost several pounds without even trying!

One week to the day of breaking up with Ben, I met Clarence...

A New Chapter

That's not entirely true. I knew Clarence. We had hung out within the same group of friends and I'd had Calculus class with him during my last year of high school. Clarence Lenting had the bluest eyes and the most amazing smile! When he smiled, his eyes and cheeks crinkled up and it looked as though his smile would eat his face. It was contagious. He was incredibly intelligent, funny, and seemed like a gentle soul. I would often find myself looking at him in Calculus and wonder why he wasn't dating anyone. How had nobody noticed this great guy and snatched him up yet? He always had very short hair (a brush cut) and I often joked around by "petting" his hair. I loved the feel of it and he said he loved it when people did that, that it gave him shivers, so I kept doing it. Sometimes I would stand behind him in the cafeteria while someone else petted his head, but he'd say, "That's not Jen," and he was always right. I asked him how he could tell the difference and he told me that nobody could mimic the way I did it, that it felt as though I was doing it with care. I guess I was.

We were just friends, but I found myself noticing him and caring about him more as the year went on. I remember one day in class, he turned to ask me a question and he had a blue shirt on. The blue in the shirt made his eyes look incredibly blue and I commented on it. I told him that was a good shirt for him and he looked really nice in it. He smiled shyly and said thanks... and wore that shirt three days a week for the rest of the school year. I loved it. I felt as though he cared about my opinion and every time he wore that shirt I was convinced he was wearing it just for me.

Everyone went their separate ways after high school. Most went to university, others to college. I stayed at home with my parents and enrolled in a one-year college program where I took Law Enforcement (Law & Security). Because I stayed home, I didn't make any really great friends the way most do when they live in a dorm with a bunch of other teens.

I met a few people I really liked, though—my favourite being Ryan. He and I clicked immediately and hung out quite a bit that year. We had a weird chemistry between us, but I had a boyfriend and he was a huge player, so that was never going to happen. Not only that, but I felt as though Ryan was out of my league. Since I felt as though I would never be with him, I did the next best thing: I matched him up with a girl at a bar one night. He noticed her from across the room and was dying to meet her. I didn't know her but said I'd make it happen for him. I introduced myself and then told her all about this great guy I knew who was funny, smart, and super cute. I asked if she'd be willing to talk to him and decide for herself, and that was that.

I don't know why girls do that, but we do. If we want a guy but feel as though we can't have him for some reason, we go out of our way to match him up with someone else. I'm writing this so that one day, should a guy stumble across this, he'll know this odd truth about women. If you're currently being pushed into a relationship by a girl you know, consider who's doing the pushing... she may just be interested herself.

Ryan and I never kept in contact after college, but I think he and the girl from the bar were still dating at that point, so who knows? They made a beautiful couple; I like to think they ended up happily ever after.

Ryan played an important role in my life. He was a great friend and he seemed to genuinely enjoy hanging out with me. His friendship helped to build up some of the self-esteem I lost while dating Ben, making it much easier for me to break up with Ben when the time came.

When the school year ended, everyone came home for the summer and I loved having all my high school friends around again. We picked up easily where we had left off. We went out as often as we could and it was during this week that I realized how incredibly happy I was to see Clarence. I hadn't even known I was missing him! University was treating him well and he had more confidence.

I confided in a mutual friend, Jay, that I was interested in Clarence, and did he think that Clarence would agree to go out with me if I asked? Jay said he was sure of it, and that's all I needed. That night I tried three different times to strike up a conversation with Clarence, to see if he would go out sometime, but every time we got interrupted or he got distracted. I took that as a sign and gave up, deciding against asking him. As we were leaving the bar, Jay asked me how it went and I said I wasn't going to try anymore. It hadn't gone well, and I was just going to accept that.

Fortunately for me, Jay *didn't* accept that. He made a point of making sure everyone had a ride home, and somehow Clarence and I just happened to be riding in the same car. As we walked toward the car, we started talking and I got over my nervousness and just blurted out, "Would you consider going out with me sometime?" I'd thought he had a beautiful smile before, but the smile he gave me as an answer was the best yet.

On our first date, we went out for dinner and then went to a park and sat on the swings. We talked for hours, covering everything from how school had gone to what we wanted to do with our lives. Where did we see ourselves realistically in five years? And again in a decade? Conversation was easy and he was so kind with me; I didn't know it was possible for a guy to be such a gentleman at that age. We were twenty years old.

When he dropped me off at the house that night, he said something that really struck a nerve with me. His dad had passed away a couple of years earlier (while I was on my exchange in Brazil), and it was evident that he'd had a huge amount of love and respect for him. He said, "If I can be half the man my dad was, I'll know that I'm a good man." I knew in that moment that Clarence wasn't like other guys our age. He had a broader view of life and a deeper regard for it. His goals were bigger than just partying at school and hopefully getting a job that would allow him to have a big house and fancy car. He was thinking of family and the kind of person he strove to be. He was doing his best to be there for his mom and little brother. This was a guy of strong character and I knew he was the kind of person I'd be lucky to spend the rest of my life with.

He must have seen something good in me, too, because by our second date we were joking about running off and getting married, but only partially joking. I think we both knew almost instantly that we had found our perfect match. For my twenty-first birthday, I spent the weekend with him in his dorm room at the University of Toronto. He didn't tell me what he had planned, but said that I should bring something nice to wear. He surprised me with a nice dinner out, followed by two tickets for us to see "Beauty and the Beast."

At the end of the performance, I looked at him and said, "I'm going to treat you so well."

He smiled. "I'm going to treat you the way you deserve to be treated."

I would have never thought I deserved to be treated like a queen, but apparently he thought so. We went back to his dorm room where he pulled out a box with a cherry cheesecake in it. Back in those days, I loved cherry cheesecake; it was my all-time favourite. He had actually borrowed someone's bicycle and rode quite a distance to get to a bakery where he heard they made amazing cheesecake, then had to balance that big box while trying to ride all the way back. He said he nearly got hit several times by cars flying by, but it was worth it to know that I would have cheesecake on my birthday.

You would think this is where I'd go on and on about how easy dating him was and that we skated right through to a blissful married life, but it didn't quite go that way.

He came home and visited me as often as he could on weekends (which made his mom crazy since she'd had his undivided attention before I came along), and I would make the trip to Toronto on the weekends I could get off from work. I had graduated from college, but was nowhere near finding a job in policing. I always passed the physical and written tests, just to make it to the interview stage where I would fall apart at the seams. At the age of twenty-one, I had little life experience and found it difficult to answer many questions. I was told several times that I was young and it might do me well to go to college or university to put in some time and gain life experience. I found that incredibly frustrating. What would I take? Police work was all I wanted to do and my tunnel vision prevented me from seeing my life any other way.

I started to job hop in an attempt to find something else I might enjoy. I ended up briefly getting a sales job and at our training session I met a guy who caught my attention. I had no desire to date anyone else and certainly wasn't looking for someone. I was perfectly happy with Clarence and the relationship we had. Little did I know that young love can be so fickle! This guy was very forward with me and made it clear that he was interested in dating me. I was young, foolish, and flattered. He said and did all the right things and suddenly I started to panic, thinking that maybe Clarence and I had gotten too serious, too soon. What if he was great but wasn't "the one"? What if I was too young to commit to someone for the rest of my life? What if this was the time in my life when I should be dating around and seeing what else was out there?

I started to distance myself from Clarence and began talking on the phone with this other guy more. Clarence came home for Valentine's weekend and had no idea that anything had changed between us. He gave me a box of chocolates and a sweet card. Seeing him in person made things more difficult. I didn't know what to do. I certainly didn't want to hurt Clarence, who had never been anything but perfect to me, but I also didn't want to lock myself into a relationship if it wasn't the right one. We went out that night and I confessed to him that I was confused about us and had developed a crush on another guy. I knew that would hurt him, but lying would have hurt him more. He said he wanted to make things work with us and he was willing to do anything, but that's the thing; he had never done anything wrong!

Things became awkward between us and he brought me home. The next night, a big group of us went out to a bar. I was joking around with a friend from high school and Clarence became clingy and jealous. It made me crazy because I had no interest whatsoever in this other guy, and if there's one thing I cannot deal with, it's a clingy guy. He was just trying to hold on to what we had, but it was having the opposite effect on me.

We all slept over at a friend's house that night and, wanting to avoid conflict, I pretended to fall asleep on the living room floor immediately. I heard Clarence talking with Jay and telling him what was going on. He confessed that he feared he was losing me and that I didn't love him anymore. Jay convinced him that I did, that I was likely confused, and that he should give me time and space. Jay was sure we would work things out. I credit Jay with helping us through one of our most difficult times together.

The next morning as I was driving Clarence home, I explained it like this: "You know how sometimes your family makes you crazy, but you don't stop loving them? You just crave a little space. Then, after having some time apart, you look forward to hanging out with them again. That's how I feel about you right now. I still think you're an amazing person, and I do love you, but you're making me crazy right now. I just need a little space, okay?"

When he got out of the car, he walked up to his mom's front door, then turned and looked at me. It breaks my heart to this day to remember this, but I saw his heart breaking as he stood there and I drove away. Seeing that expression on his face, and knowing that I had caused it, did something to me. I wanted desperately to turn around and beg him to forgive me, but something held me back. I just needed to be sure. I knew that I had to make a decision and it had to be final; I couldn't play around with his emotions like that. I lay in bed that night not knowing what to do. Should I stay with Clarence? Should I date this new guy? Should I remain single for a while? A few things would happen this particular night to change the direction of my life.

I went to bed feeling tormented, as if this would be the biggest decision of my life. I guess at that time, it was. I couldn't sleep. Finally, I did something I had never done before—I called out to God in desperation. I felt as though I needed help making such a big decision, and somehow it just felt right to ask God. I guess you could say that this became my first "God story."

I felt an intense urge to call the other guy. I suddenly felt as though it was very important that I talk to him. I tiptoed downstairs so as not to wake my parents or sister, and called him. We talked for nearly an hour and then he asked me what my boyfriend's name was. He knew I had a boyfriend, but I had never said his name. I asked why it mattered to him and he said, "I just want to know. Come on, tell me."

"Okay," I said. "It's Clarence."

Then he started to laugh. He laughed so hard that he could hardly breathe. Then he proceeded to make fun of Clarence's name.

After hearing that, so many things became clear to me. First, I realized that there are a lot of guys in this world who look perfect on the surface. They say and do the right things, and they may even be attractive, but the truly great guys are great all the time and to everyone, not just to those they are trying to impress. Secondly, I knew in my heart that Clarence would never have done that to someone else. He would never have made fun of a person, especially over something they had no control over. Finally, I learned that this praying to God thing—it may just be something I could get into.

The next day, I drove to Clarence's mom's place and knocked on the door. Clarence answered and looked as though he hadn't slept at all. I told him that I hadn't stopped thinking about us and that I knew what I wanted to do. If he could forgive me for hurting him and for almost ending things, then I wanted to stay with him. I wanted to make things work and I wanted to never let anything like that happen to us again. He gave me a big hug and said he'd been hoping I felt that way. We continued dating, but it was different this time—we were more focused, more committed, and happier than ever.

I had applied to the RCMP (Royal Canadian Mounted Police) and passed both the first written test and physical (I'm happy to say that I passed the physical before they made it easier for women). I had an interview coming up and Clarence and I were nervous about it. What if this time I had a good interview? I would have to go to Regina, Saskatchewan for six months of training. How would we deal with that separation?

My birthday is in March and a month beforehand, I had a sense that Clarence was thinking about proposing. We were hanging out in my parents' basement one night and I asked him if that was the case. He smiled nervously and I started to cry. He asked what was wrong.

"I don't want you to propose," I said, then cried harder.

I cried so hard I could barely breathe. I didn't know how I was ever going to explain to him the way I was feeling. I don't know how he knew, but he just did.

"It's okay, I get it," he said. "You don't want me to propose right now—but that doesn't mean you don't want me to propose ever, is that it?"

Yes! That was exactly it! We were twenty-one and I still felt a little freaked out at the thought of being engaged and married so young, but I did know that he was the one I wanted to marry. He truly seemed to understand and told me not to worry, that he would wait until the time was right. The crazy thing is, once I knew he wasn't going to propose and that pressure was removed, that's when I felt comfortable with the idea of marrying him.

My birthday came and went on March 26, and as promised, no ring. I then knew what I wanted to get him for his birthday. He had been born just after me, on April 7. That particular year, his birthday fell on Easter. I bought a stuffed rabbit, removed the body soap that its arms were wrapped around, and instead bought a simple gold ring. I placed the ring box in the rabbit's arms.

I'll never forget his birthday. I wasn't sure when to give him his gift exactly, but I knew I wanted to be alone with him. We were at his mom's place and finally I said, "Will you come outside with me?"

We went out to the driveway and I made him close his eyes while I got his gift from the car. I handed him the rabbit and said, "I'm not sure how you want to take this. I don't know how this interview will turn out, but I want this ring to remind you that no matter how it goes, and no matter where I am, I consider myself to be with you—permanently."

Clarence ran straight into the house and yelled, "Mom! Mom! Jen just proposed to *me!*"

I wasn't sure if it was a proposal or not, but I suppose at that point, it was! I went home that night and told my mom, "I think I just got engaged.'

You've probably already guessed it: I bombed the interview.

Clarence was about to start his second year at U of T, but his heart wasn't in it. He had thought he would become a pharmacist, but he wasn't enjoying university. He wasn't getting any practical or hands-on learning and he didn't look forward to going to class. We were convinced we would be married one day and I said that when I married him, his debt would become my debt as well. I didn't mind having debt, but not for years spent partying at university if he wasn't going to come out of it with a job that he was good at and enjoyed. He switched over last minute and applied to Conestoga College, where he took the paramedic program. At that time, it was a one-year program. He loved it immediately.

I was still bouncing from job to job, trying to get hired onto a police force. Clarence saw a job for security guards in the Kitchener/Guelph area and suggested I apply for that. At least then we could live closer to each other. I applied and was hired. This company trained us to work with guard dogs and sent us into sketchy locations in and around the Toronto area to patrol various buildings, truck yards, parking lots, etc. It was boring work and nothing ever happened, but working with the Dobermans was fun. That job convinced me that if I ever got a dog, I wanted it to be a Doberman. They were so smart and had so much character!

I remember being incredibly sick one night but couldn't call in sick because there was nobody available to cover for me. I picked up my dog and headed to the building I was supposed to patrol. I had a high fever, body sweats, and couldn't stop shivering. What I ended up doing was staying in my car all night wrapped up in a blanket. I must have fallen asleep at some point and awoke to someone banging on my window. I rolled it down and saw a security guard from another company. When he asked if I was okay, I explained that I was supposed to be working, but I was so sick that all I could do was just try to get through the shift.

"It looks as though your dog is sick, too," he said.

I turned to see Boomer sprawled on his back, with all four legs in the air and his tongue hanging out the side of his mouth. The other guard told me to take care and lock my doors as they did a drive through of the parking lot to make sure everything was okay.

Once he walked away, I looked at Boomer again and whispered, "Boomer?"

I'm not kidding when I say he opened one eye, and when he saw we were alone, he jumped into an upright position with what looked like a huge smile on his face. He then started to kiss my cheek! Yes, some day I would own a Doberman of my own.

Missed Opportunities
and Mixed Blessings

A teacher announced to Clarence's class at school that there would be a couple of openings for ambulance dispatchers in the Kitchener/Cambridge area and suggested that students apply. They said that it could be difficult to get a job and that some people had better luck becoming dispatchers first before transferring over to become paramedics. Clarence told me I should apply as well. I didn't know why, since that wasn't my chosen career path, but I told him I'd go along and write the tests with him. It could be fun and we could compare notes at the end.

Hundreds of people showed up to write the test. What we never expected was that we both got a call saying we were in the top fifty. Did we want to come out for the second level of testing and an interview? We were ecstatic! We did the testing and the interview on the same day and I felt pretty good about it. So did Clarence. I didn't think I had gotten the job, but I didn't embarrass myself, and all those police interviews had come in handy because I was finally able to answer their questions intelligently. I was shocked, though, when I got a call stating that I had been chosen for the Cambridge area. Clarence was second, meaning that if I didn't accept the position, they would offer it to him. What a crazy position to be put in!

I didn't know what to do, but he said I should go for it. In a few months, he would be graduating and he really wanted to be a paramedic. I accepted and was sent off for training where I was put up in a hotel with my meals paid for. I even got paid the entire time I was in class. I had never had a job where I made so much money! I felt as though I had won the lottery.

The other people in training were very nice and we all got along well. One night they were all going to the bar for drinks and invited me along. I went and made a terrible mistake while I was there. I forgot who I was with. I had never been taught the very important lesson of, "When you first get a job, you need to remember for the first six months to a year that you are *new*. Keep your thoughts to yourself until you understand the way things work, not just the work."

The trainers were talking about their lives, kids, etc. and I started chatting along as though I was one of them. Here I was, a twenty-two-year-old kid who thought she knew everything about everything, and I suggested to one of the trainers that maybe she had her daughter enrolled in too many extracurricular activities. By the way she described it, her daughter sounded exhausted from everything she was involved with. The trainer looked at me, very clearly annoyed, and said that she was quite capable of parenting her daughter and that her daughter loved doing all those things. I knew immediately that I had spoken out of turn and kept my thoughts to myself after that, but the damage was done.

When we wrote our final exams, we had to get an eighty percent score or higher on each of them or we wouldn't get the job. I got in the eighties on all of them except two. I got seventy-eight percent on one and seventy-six on the other. I literally missed them by a couple of questions. I knew that I wasn't the only one. I heard one of the men say that he didn't get eighty percent on one of his. We were each called into a room individually where they would let us know what our next steps were. Everyone was coming back to the room stating that they had been hired, even the guy who failed a test, so I figured I would be okay. I went into the room and they told me that, unfortunately, they would have to rescind the offer.

I felt so foolish that I couldn't even look at anyone. I knew that I had brought this upon myself and there was no going back. I thought about all the people I had bragged to about getting this awesome new job, and how humiliating it would be to have to admit that I had lost it.

I started to cry uncontrollably. My shame felt like too much to bear. One of the trainers called Clarence and asked if he could come pick me up; they didn't think I was in any state to drive. I waited in my hotel room and wanted to die when Clarence came in. I had failed. I had lct us down. Not only that, but *he* would not have made the mistakes I had made. He would have been great at that job and I'd blocked him from getting it, just to lose it myself.

I apologized profusely for what I had done and Clarence just sat and held me while I cried. I told him that I couldn't leave while everyone was still downstairs, that I couldn't face my family and friends after this, and that I would save my money and head to Brazil. I knew I always had a place there, and I could always teach English.

He made me look at him. "You're not a failure," he said. "And you're not going to Brazil! This job was never you. You're not defined by your job and you're an amazing person. Those people were lucky to get to meet you. Now walk out of here with your head high and know that what I'm saying is true."

I didn't necessarily believe it, but what I did know was that Clarence was someone I could trust. He was someone I could fail in front of and he wouldn't judge or abandon me. He would protect my heart and defend my honour. He was a good man.

While this may not be one of my "God stories," per se, I wholly believe that God had His hand in the mix.

Just a few months later, Clarence graduated. That same week, he got a call from the ambulance base in Forest offering him a permanent part-time position. We had decided that we wouldn't get married until at least one of us had a permanent position that paid well. He accepted the offer immediately, then turned to look at me and said, "Pick a date, we're getting married."

We wasted no time. He graduated at the end of May and we were married on July 12 of that same year, 1997. Had I gotten that job in Cambridge, there's no way I would have wanted to leave it to move to Forest. As embarrassing as it was, I truly believe that everything worked out the way it did for a reason.

We had a small wedding in a park with twenty-five people in attendance. We were twenty-two years old. When the ceremony was over and the papers were signed, we turned toward our parents and said, "Now what?"

I'm sure people thought we wouldn't last more than a year. We knew otherwise.

Married Life
and Life Lessons

We hadn't been married very long when I drove from Forest to Strathroy one day. It was a beautiful, sunny day and I was in a good mood. All of the sudden, all sorts of strange thoughts started to race through my mind. I recalled every poor choice I had made, every bad decision, every failed attempt, the look on Clarence's face when I had left him standing on his doorstep—all of it came rushing around me and I started to feel as though I was drowning. As I was driving, I said, "God, if you can hear me, I hope you can forgive me for all these things I've done, because I don't know if I can."

In that moment, I felt an incredible weight being lifted. If I had ever doubted God before, I most certainly believed in Him now. Nothing anyone could have said to me that day would have taken all the pain away. No amount of reason or reassurance could have set everything straight. I knew then that He had heard my prayer and felt my anguish—and forgiven me. I had called out to Him once before and He had prompted me to get out of bed and make a call. This time, He responded just as quickly but required me to do nothing. He didn't ask me to do a single thing; He just took that weight from me because I asked. I had a hard time comprehending that and felt as though I must owe Him something, but I wasn't made to feel that way at all. This is one of my favourite God stories. I arrived home feeling like a new person.

Speaking of "home," we lived in a two-bedroom apartment on the third floor of a walk-up. We had a bed and dresser, but no furniture beyond that. We had a small seventeen-inch television that sat on a green box. We laid out blankets on the living room floor and had picnic-style meals there, lying down on pillows and blankets to watch TV. We loved it. People tried to give us their old hand-me-downs for furniture, but we decided we were happy with the little to nothing we had. We worked hard and saved our money to buy things one piece at a time, as we could afford them.

When we finally did have some money saved, we ended up buying a weight bench and free-weights so we could turn our spare bedroom into a small workout room. Having something to do in this small town, which seemed to become a ghost town at about 6:30 p.m. each night, was more important to us than having furniture. Our friends who were just as broke as we were all chipped in and bought us some plastic chairs and a small plastic table as a wedding gift —which we broke out for guests whenever they came over. It was a simple life but we loved it, and we loved each other.

Clarence was the only part-timer in Forest, so any time someone went on vacation or used sick time, he got those hours. He tended to get lots of hours in the summer months and not so many in the winter. We became good at saving all our money because we didn't always know when the next round of shifts would come. I found work immediately at the front desk of the Forest Golf and Country Hotel. I was paid a little more than minimum wage and worked the 3:00–11:00 p.m. shift. My coworkers were lots of fun. There were no hours for me in the winter months, though, so I applied around and got a job as a cashier at Knechtel's Grocery Store. It was okay, but I was surprised by how many muscles I pulled after my first few days; sliding, lifting, and bagging items all day takes a surprising toll on the body.

There was a cashier there who had been hoping that a friend of hers would get hired, and when they hired me instead she decided that she hated me. I had never met this lady before, but she was miserable with me from the moment we first met.

It didn't take long for me to realize that when I got really stressed, I developed flu-like symptoms. Every time I stepped foot in that store, I suffered from instant headaches, sore throats, and an upset stomach. By the time I got home after my shift (about a two-minute car ride), I would feel perfectly fine. It's amazing how one person can ruin your life, but this lady seemed to get a great deal of pleasure out of trying to ruin mine. I stuck it out, though, and refused to let her get the best of me.

There were a few issues weighing on me. I worked at a job I didn't care about and got bullied nearly every shift. I lived in a very small town where everyone seemed to know each other, but it was hard to break into any of the social circles. Nobody ever visited us, with the exception of Clarence's best friend Brad, who would come from Toronto when he could. In the nearly three years we lived there, I think my parents showed up twice.

I didn't explain this earlier, but something changed between my mom and me the day I moved out of my parents' home. I'm not sure what happened or how exactly, but something in our relationship broke and we never seemed to make it right. She never called or visited me while I lived in Kitchener, and being the stubborn person I am, I returned the favour.

During this time in my life, I became closer with my dad again. He was no longer running the garbage company but had started trucking. He would call me anytime he was passing by, just to let me know he wasn't far from me and he was thinking of me. We had fun chats and I lived for those calls.

When Clarence worked, he was gone for twelve-hour shifts. During busy times, I found myself feeling incredibly alone in the world. I started to have a hard time getting out of bed, and basically didn't unless I had to go to work. I could wake up for that, but then I would immediately go to bed upon returning home. I had no energy for anything and it got so bad that I thought I might have mono.

I made an appointment to see my family doctor to see if she could help me. We chatted for a bit and then she asked me what was wrong. I told her I thought I was suffering from mono and she said, "Do you think you may be a little depressed?"

I laughed and said, "No!" Then I burst into tears.

She asked what was going on and I explained how lonely I felt, how much I hated my work, and that I was living in a new town and I had nothing. She said it was no wonder I was feeling this way and gave me ten days' worth of Paxil. She told me to make an appointment if I didn't notice a change after the ten days had passed.

I went home feeling oddly relieved. I wasn't crazy! I felt as though she had validated my feelings and that she was going to help me shake this funk I was in. When Clarence got home that night, we sat on the bed and I told him what my doctor had said. We had a long talk about everything and he asked what would make me happy. I didn't know exactly, I just knew that I was spinning my wheels in this place. He said that he would do whatever it took to make me happy; he wanted to help.

I then confided something in him that I had been carrying around for as long as I could remember. I had never shared this with anyone. I told him that ever since I'd been a little girl, I had a feeling that I would die by the time I was thirty years old. Unlike most teenagers or early twenty-somethings, I never felt as though thirty was "old." It always seemed close to me and each birthday left me feeling a little more anxious.

"Do you think that maybe you can't envision yourself living beyond thirty because you've never set any goals for yourself that would bring you beyond that point?" he asked. "Your biggest goal until now has been to become a police officer, but even if you did accomplish that, you most likely would have been in your mid-twenties. Then what? What do you have to work toward?"

He suggested that I consider going back to school. These low-paying, part-time, go-nowhere jobs left me feeling antsy and un-fulfilled. I had no idea what I wanted to do, though, and policing no longer interested me. He suggested that I talk to a counsellor at the local high school and pick up some books from colleges and universities; we could go through them together and see if anything looked good.

I met with a nice man at the local school who was very en-couraging and gave me all sorts of material. Clarence and I looked through local newspapers to see who was hiring and for what. We narrowed it down to two fields—accounting or computer program-ming. I would be pretty much guaranteed to find a job when I gradu-ated from either of those two fields.

I started taking the pills I was given and things turned around almost immediately. I felt as though I had much more energy, so I started jogging. My mood changed drastically for the better.

While working at the grocery store one day, a friendly lady came up to my counter. I started chatting with her as I scanned her groceries and she mentioned that she worked at the local Royal Bank. I told her that I was considering going back to school to study accounting. We made a little more small talk and she said, "You know, we could use a part-timer at the bank. You should consider applying."

It had never occurred to me to apply at a bank before, but I figured I might as well, so I applied. What I didn't know was that she was actually the manager at that bank. I was hired within a few weeks. I only took seven of those pills, and somehow I knew that I would never need them again.

It gave me great pleasure to quit my job at the grocery store. I'm not particularly proud of this now, but at the time it gave me an even greater amount of pleasure to tell that other cashier off just before I left. I must have been overheard by someone, because the next time I returned there to shop, former coworkers came up to me and whispered that they'd heard what I'd done. They wanted to thank me! Apparently she had made more lives awful than just mine.

I loved my job at the bank! I made ten dollars per hour and it was the first time I had broken into double digits (with the exception of my dispatch training, where I'd made more than double that). Clarence bought me a gold chain with a small diamond pendant as a "congratulations" for starting my first professional job. It was crazy how proud of me he was. I absolutely loved everyone who worked there and each one treated me better than the next.

I was about to apply to various colleges when my boss Melissa asked if she could see me in her office. Along with Bob, our financial advisor, she sat me down and asked if I was still considering applying to an accounting program. I said I was and they both suggested that I reconsider. They said I was much more of a people person than a number-cruncher and they were convinced that I wouldn't like the field, that I'd be miserable. They asked what else I was considering.

"There's a Computer Programmer Analyst program at Lambton College," I said, "but to be honest, I don't know much about computers."

They both agreed that I should go for it anyway. Every job required some sort of computer experience, and even if I didn't become a programmer, having a computer background would open more doors for me. I had a lot of respect for both of them and was grateful that my employers took such a great interest in me that they would try to prevent me from making a bad decision. Clarence and I talked about it and he agreed with them. I sent off my application and waited nervously for a reply.

A Time for Change

I got in! In September of 1999, I walked into the beginning of what would be a three-and-a-half-year program, including co-op work terms. I remember coming home feeling terrified because I didn't speak the lingo. The other students all seemed to know everything about RAM, ROM, and a million other acronyms, but I had no idea what any of it meant.

Clarence sat me down and said, "Jen, you learned to read, write, and speak another language in one year. This is just another language, that's all. You don't have to know it all at once. You have more than three years to take it all in."

When he put it like that, it seemed very doable and I became determined to not only pass, but graduate near the top of my class. We didn't tell anyone in my family that I was in school. I was sure they already looked at me as a failure since I'd wanted to become a police officer for so long and never succeeded. My opportunity to become a dispatcher hadn't gone any better. I wasn't sure I would enjoy this program or do well at it, but I sure didn't feel like adding it to my growing list of failures.

I finished my first year with a 3.96 GPA and was still working at both the bank and the hotel. I knew once I made it through my first year that I would make it through the program. After all, our class had already seen more than a third of the people fail or drop out. I studied hard and was determined, so I had the confidence to carry on until the end of the program.

After my first year, Clarence and I took my parents out to dinner and told them the news—that I was back in school and had just completed my first year with flying colours. I think they were a little hurt that I hadn't let them in on it from the beginning, but they were happy for me just the same. Because I didn't see my family very often, I didn't feel particularly close to them and I didn't feel the need to explain or apologize.

Clarence was growing tired of taking lots of shifts, but only in spurts, and there was no full-time position in sight. He thought he might be able to get another part-time position in Sarnia to fill some of the empty spaces when he wasn't working. He applied and got hired. They said they didn't have a lot of shifts at first, but he would get some. That worked out perfectly for him—or so he thought. He mentioned to his boss that he had accepted another part-time position, but that he would get very few shifts and that his current job was still his first priority. His boss was furious with him and acted as though Clarence had betrayed him. Clarence reiterated that this job would come first and he would make sure to fill shifts here before accepting any in Sarnia. It didn't matter. In retaliation, his boss hired a second part-timer and began giving shifts to him instead. It was very hurtful.

We spent the first three years of our marriage in Forest and met some great people there. We were getting comfortable and trying to make a life for ourselves ... but with Clarence's new problems at work it felt as though the rug had been pulled out from under us. Clarence was really disappointed and worried about how we would pay our bills if he couldn't get enough shifts. I may not have known much at that age, but I knew one thing: no man was going to rule over our lives and well-being. We didn't intend to live under this man's thumb, having him decide if we had money to pay the rent that month or not. I told Clarence in no uncertain terms that we were leaving this town—immediately. I was attending school in Sarnia and he now had a part-time job there, so it made sense for us to move. I wasn't worried about paying the bills. I wasn't afraid to take on another job, and if I had to work the night shift at Wendy's, that was what I would do. Clarence gave his notice at the Forest ambulance base and we moved within the month.

The next few years passed in a happy blur. School went well and I had three really great co-op experiences. I learned a lot during that time. About a year and a half into the program, I was still working at the bank, but I decided it was time to leave my job at the hotel. Not long after that, Clarence mentioned that there was a posting at Strathroy Hospital for a patient registration clerk in the Emergency Department. I didn't really think I would land a job at a hospital, but I applied and it turned out that they liked that I had a computer background and lots of customer service experience. I got the job. I made over seventeen dollars per hour and couldn't believe my good fortune!

I absolutely loved that job. I had great coworkers, the doctors and nurses in emergency were easy to work with, and I made more money than I had ever made before to do a job I truly enjoyed. I always told Clarence how lucky we were. He'd look at me and say, "Not lucky, Jen. Blessed."

We had gotten into a routine of reading a little bit out of the Bible each night before going to bed. Sometimes the stories would bore me, but I loved having that togetherness with him.

After being married for three years, we took our first trip together. A honeymoon! We went to Panama and had a fantastic time. We loved it so much that we decided this was something that needed to happen more often. We started taking a trip a year, and then two.

My second co-op term had me working at Lambton College. The person I was supposed to report to was rarely around, so I ended up reporting to Terry instead. This, I believe, was a God thing. Terry loved talking about God, church, religion, and anything else that a person might be open to talking about. He began to ask about my childhood, my husband, my school experience, and finally my beliefs. I told him that I believed in God, and I think I always had. As a young girl, I'd had a childlike faith and my prayers basically went something like this: "Dear God, I know I should have studied for that test yesterday, and I promise I'll study for the next one, but if you could just help me pass this one, that would be really great." Then I would get the test back with a big A on it and be sure that God had helped. My prayers may not have been very deep or meaningful, but I somehow always felt that He was hearing them just the same.

It was only as I entered my teen years, and became incredibly prideful in thinking I could make all my own decisions and be fine, that I started to part ways with God. I didn't really think about Him at all. Church bored me and I found it very hypocritical. We would sit through a sermon about how we needed to be good people, and then the sermon would end and we'd go downstairs for "coffee hour" where I would wolf down juice and cookies and listen to the adults trash-talk each other behind their backs. I hated it there, and as soon as I had a job I began taking shifts on Sundays so I wouldn't have to attend anymore. I guess you could say that I was blocked from seeing God by all of the "good" people.

Terry seemed to know lots about God and faith and I had some questions that hadn't ever been answered during my years in church and Sunday school. For example, I didn't understand how awful people, such as murderers and rapists in jail, could claim that they had found Jesus and then suddenly be accepted by God and allowed into Heaven. That bothered me. Terry explained that there's no grey area when it comes to sin. It's black and white—sin is sin. There aren't levels of sin—it's all bad in God's eyes. If I had ever lied, stolen, coveted other people's things, used God's name in vain, worshipped other gods, not honoured my mother and father, etc., then I was no better than the murderer or rapist I had just described. He explained that this was the beauty of it all. In comparison to God's holy perfection, we all look dirty and pitiful. The fact that God's love and forgiveness is available to anyone who seeks it, that we can't be too low or dirty to ask for His forgiveness and receive it—well, this was great news!

I don't know if I fully comprehended what Terry said, but Clarence and I went out for dinner that night and I shared the details of this conversation with him.

"It sounds as though this guy knows what he's talking about," Clarence said. "He must be getting his information from some-where—ask him which church he attends and maybe we should check it out for ourselves."

That's how Clarence and I started attending Temple Baptist Church in Sarnia. Terry also introduced me to some women who were in need of extra players for their volleyball team, so I began to play with them. Then he invited Clarence and I to join the small group that he and his wife belonged to. We had never belonged to a small group before and weren't quite sure what that meant, but basically we got together once every other week with a group of people, rotating between all of our houses. We met some nice couples and started to feel as though we had connections in this church.

This small group continued to invite new couples to join and eventually it became too big—nobody had a house big enough to comfortably host that many people. It was decided that the group should split into two. Clarence and I were nervous because we liked everyone, but for obvious reasons we felt closer to Terry and his wife, and there were two other couples we seemed to really click with. Nonetheless, it started to look as though we wouldn't end up in their group and, while we liked everyone else, we had less in common with them. We weren't sure what to do and whether or not we should just bow out altogether. Could we do that without looking like jerks?

Then something amazing happened; two of the men approached us one Sunday after church and said, "We need to talk to you. We're trying to split these groups evenly so that everyone is happy, and we're having a difficult time deciding where you fit in. There's a new small group forming that's younger than us. They're all your age. None of them have children, like you, and they have similar careers. We think you would fit in nicely with them. Would you consider joining this group?"

We said we would, and they introduced us to these younger couples. This would turn out to be a huge blessing as these would come to be some of our closest friends. In a few short years, we would even take a trip to Cuba with two of the couples in this group.

I graduated from Lambton College with a Computer Programmer Analyst diploma and realized that the computer field wasn't as easy to break into as I had been led to believe. There were a lot of brilliant programmers out there and, while I enjoyed programming, I wasn't particularly good at it.

Clarence had taken yet another part-time paramedic position in Chatham and the very first week he worked there, they posted a full-time position in Wallaceburg, which was much closer to where we lived. He wasn't going to apply for it because he had only worked one shift, but a coworker pulled him aside and said that he should send a note and a resume to the manager. He did, and sure enough, the position was his! His first full-time permanent position! We were beside ourselves with excitement.

Since I didn't really have a career to speak of and seemed to have the ability to find part-time work anywhere I went, and since Clarence was now going to be working full-time, he thought it might be nice to move closer to Wallaceburg so he wouldn't have such a long drive. I agreed, but refused to move any closer than Corunna. We didn't intend to build a house, but everything seemed to move so quickly… before we knew it, we had signed the paperwork and watched a huge hole get dug into the ground where our very own beautiful home would be.

One day I got a call from the college stating that Labatt Breweries was seeking a person to work at their computer helpdesk, and would I be interested in an interview? I jumped at the opportunity. With years of customer service jobs behind me—and many, many interviews—I nailed this one. They offered me the position. What's amazing to me is that they hadn't picked my resume out of the list when they initially went through them. They had chosen to interview other people, but one of them had already accepted a position elsewhere, so they asked Judy, who worked at the college assisting students looking for co-op positions and jobs, if she could recommend someone to them. She told them that she was surprised they hadn't picked my resume, and they should interview me as well. They told me this at the end of my interview, and that they were grateful she had pointed them in my direction. For that, Judy received all of my gratitude, and a huge bouquet of flowers.

The drive from our apartment in Sarnia to Labatt in London took about an hour. A few months later, our house was completed and we moved to Corunna, making my drive an hour and a half. That made my eight-hour days more like eleven or twelve, depending on whether I would get out of work on time and how traffic was. I loved that job and met some incredible people, so it seemed well worth it.

To break up the drive, I would stay overnight at my parents' place once a week, since work was only a half-hour from their house. This also helped me reconnect with them. Clarence was working full-time in Wallaceburg and on his days off he took part-time shifts in Sarnia-Lambton, working at various bases throughout the county. He loved everything about his job and became very close with many of his coworkers, especially Ken, who was his permanent partner in Wallaceburg.

I loved my work and made decent money. We were careful with our income and placed a lot of importance on saving it. We made our own lunches rather than buying them at work, we ate most of our meals at home rather than eating out, we didn't spend money on things like smoking or drinking, and then once or twice a year we would treat ourselves to awesome vacations in sunny locales.

We rarely if ever fought, which seemed odd to us. Everyone had told us how hard marriage was and that it was a lot of work; we were supposedly going to go through some rough times, but we weren't seeing it. During our first year of marriage, we figured we had been fight-free because we were newlyweds, and we braced ourselves for year two. Year two came and went, and while I dealt with being depressed for a time and there were some big changes as I hopped from one job to another and returned to school, there was never any turmoil between us. We figured year three must be the devastating year, but that, too, passed with ease. Sometimes we felt so odd about not fighting that we would make up pretend fights and "have it out" with each other, but even those would end with hysterical laughter. I came to the conclusion that all those people who said that it was "all downhill after marriage" were simply doing it wrong. Aaaahhhh, to be young and naïve.

My first year at Labatt was fantastic. In my second year, I was given more responsibility but stayed at the helpdesk. In year three, I applied to a different position within the company. I was all about proving myself and climbing the corporate ladder. It was during this time that I would learn one of my biggest life lessons. The position I took was called "Client Services" and I was responsible for creating and removing computer user accounts. Basically, if you were new at the company or moving to a different job role, I would set up all your computer applications, make sure you had the right amount of access to the applications you used, and remove you from them if you left that role or the company. It seemed like a straightforward enough position and I worked at it alongside one other woman.

I hated this job with a passion. I thought it would be a great move for me because it moved me to the third floor, where much of management worked, and it distanced me from the "lowly" helpdesk position. What I realized very quickly was that I *am* helpdesk. That's who I am; it's what I do best. In this new role, I rarely needed to talk to other people, so I stayed in my cubicle all day long and felt as though I was withering away. Not only that, but my coworker misunderstood why I was working so hard. I was new to the role and wanted to prove that I could do it well, but she saw me as competitive and thought I was trying to upstage her. That wasn't the case, but sometimes peoples' perception becomes their truth and she hated me almost immediately.

There I was, stuck in this cubicle doing a job I hated beside a woman who hated me, and suddenly the drive to and from work began to feel *very* long. I desperately wanted my old job back, but I learned an important lesson: you can't go back. You can always move up the ladder, but if you go one step too far, that's where you'll stay. The step beneath you has already been filled and you either stay where you are or jump off the ladder.

I decided I had to do something to prepare myself to leave this place, because I knew I couldn't stay forever. I began taking some university courses at King's College and volunteered at the London Distress Centre. I figured the volunteer work would give me some new experiences—and it would look good on my resume. The calls I received while at the Distress Centre were eye-opening. I started to see for the first time just how much hurt and illness there is in the world.

During these three years with Labatt, my home life was great and Clarence and I developed great relationships with the other couples in our small group. I learned a lot about God, who He really is, and lots about myself and who I really am.

Because I was driving three hours a day to and from work, I knew every song in every genre that was ever played on the radio. A new Christian station had recently formed and I thought I would give it a chance since I already had every possible dance, rock, rap, and country song memorized. The station was Power 88.3. They only played a few songs over and over again, but I really liked them and enjoyed listening to this station for a change. After listening to it for about a month, I began to tire of those few songs and thought I would switch back to the dance/Top 40 stuff I usually listened to. The only problem was the banter between the songs. I had gotten used to 88.3, where the commercials were actually interesting; the banter wasn't great, but it was short and uplifting. When I switched back to my old station, I realized just how rude and obnoxious the banter was. It seems every deejay on every station was looking to make a name for him or herself by catering to the masses. The problem? When you want to appeal to the largest number of people, you have to cater to the lowest common denominator. I decided that I didn't want to be part of the lowest common denominator anymore and switched back to the Christian station.

Not only that, but I realized just how much my moods were affected by music. After listening to rap or rock for ninety minutes, I would arrive at work in a good mood, but ready for a good fight at the same time. When I arrived after listening to ninety minutes of Christian music, I was in a good mood and felt a real sense of lightheartedness and willingness to deal with peoples' problems in a calm manner. The more I took in this music, the more I actually started to like myself. It became addictive! To this day, this is the music I listen to the most.

Good Decisions,
Bad Decisions,
and the Biggest Decision

One morning, I experienced something I had never experienced before. This would mark a turning point in my life. Clarence was working the night shift, so I was home alone. It was early in the morning (probably around 5:00 a.m.)—a time that nobody should have to be awake and a time that I would *never* wake up on my own.

I had what you could call a dream, but this was like no dream I'd ever had. I think of it as more of a vision—that's the best way I can describe it. All of a sudden, I was surrounded by an incredibly bright light and warmth. Picture lying in the hot sun by a pool where the temperature is perfect; it's not muggy at all, just warm and relaxing. You can hear the soft waves and every muscle in your body relaxes. Your eyes are closed and the sun shining on your face is warm and inviting. Now multiply that feeling of warmth, light, and soothing relaxation by about a million. That's how amazing I felt.

Just then, I saw Jesus off in the distance. It was strange because He seemed to be quite a distance away and I couldn't make out specific details about His face or appearance other than that He was wearing a white robe—but somehow I just knew it was Him. As far away as He appeared, His voice sounded as though He was speaking right into my ear.

"Will you follow Me?" He asked.

There was no need to think about how to answer—who wouldn't want to follow Him if it meant staying in this place?

"Yes," I said.

"Will you follow Me freely?"

"Anywhere."

I woke up immediately, practically bouncing out of bed and into the shower. I remember singing the song "God of Wonders" while in the shower at the top of my lungs. I literally floated on air as I got ready for work that morning.

Then it hit me… Clarence! I felt as though God was asking if I would follow Him, and I'd said yes. I'd said I would follow Him freely, and I understood in that moment that it meant I would have to leave everyone and everything behind while I did so. But I hadn't thought about how I would say my goodbyes. I was convinced that God was going to take my life that day. Knowing how amazing it felt to be near Him, I wasn't concerned about that, but I had no idea how I was going to communicate this to my best friend and biggest supporter—my husband.

I thought about picking up the phone and calling him before he left work to say goodbye, but I didn't know what exactly to say and I was worried he might hear something strange in my voice and worry about me. I didn't want him to worry. I decided instead to leave a note. This would be something he could read and reread if he needed to. I thanked him for the date night we had shared recently and let him know how much I loved spending time with him. I told him that he had always been nothing but amazing to me and I loved him deeply, and to remember that—forever. Then I signed it, took one last look around the house, and headed out.

Now, I may have been ready to meet my maker, but that didn't mean I was looking forward to the way in which it might happen. At every light, I looked carefully both ways, wondering where the car would come from that would ultimately hit me and take my life. Obviously, I didn't get struck and killed on my way to work. About an hour after I arrived, I got a call from Clarence. He had arrived at home and read my letter.

"Jen, I don't want you to take this the wrong way, but… were you drinking this morning before you left for work?"

I laughed and assured him I had not been drinking. He asked why I had left such a loving letter and ended it as though he wouldn't see me again. I apologized for scaring him and said it was sort of an odd story, but I would share it with him in detail when I got home. Of course, I didn't really believe that I would be making it home that night. We said "I love you" and I finished out the rest of my workday, making sure to say goodbye to everyone before I left.

Then... I made it home.

I was confused because I was certain that I had understood that vision correctly, that I would be leaving behind everything that was important to me to follow Jesus, and yet He didn't take me. I told Clarence about it in great detail and we tried to figure out what it may have meant, but we just didn't know. We shared it with our small group that week.

"That's cool," one of the girls said. "I wish I could have an experience like that!"

I didn't understand why she thought it was cool since nothing really came of it.

"Don't you see?" she asked. "God has called you and given you the opportunity to answer in such a clear way. I wish I would have the opportunity to hear His voice and answer His call like that."

I still didn't completely understand, but in time I would.

There were rumours that our IT department was going to be outsourced and the stress level in the building rose exponentially. I feel as though my last year there aged me about ten years. Gas prices rose and it started to feel as though I wasn't making enough money for it to be worth the commute anymore. I needed out.

I started to apply for anything and everything and ended up getting an office job in Sarnia. The pay was next to nothing, but I would only be driving twenty minutes as opposed to an hour and a half, meaning I'd actually be home by dinner time. I wouldn't be so exhausted all the time. I jumped at the opportunity.

What I actually did, though, was jump from my sinking ship right into the turbulent waters. If I thought I knew stress at Labatt, it paled in comparison to working at this office. The morale in the office was nonexistent, the expectations of the staff were unreal, and this wasn't even close to what I had envisioned myself doing. I lasted there exactly three months before handing in my resignation. My boss was as eager to see me go as I was to leave. We left on good terms, agreeing that this job simply wasn't a good fit for me. This was the first time in my life I ever left a job without having another job waiting for me. I was sure I'd find something quickly, but a week turned into two, which turned into three, and I started to become nervous.

I became so depressed at the poor decision I had made that I began to drink. I would wait for my neighbours to get home and we'd hang out in their garage talking, laughing, and drinking. I remember Clarence coming home one Saturday after a long day of work and seeing me sitting outside drinking—no dinner ready, the house was a mess, and I acted as though I didn't have a care in the world. We went into the house together and he called me out on my behaviour.

"Hey, just because I don't have a job right now, that doesn't mean I can't celebrate the weekend like everyone else," I told him.

He just shook his head and sighed. He really was too patient with me. (In all honesty, though, I still think that was a funny reply.)

I did have a few interviews before leaving my office job, but I hadn't heard back from any of them. One interview was for a desktop position (helpdesk with legs, as I like to explain it) at a company called NOVA Chemicals. This would have been a dream job as the pay was great and it was right down the road from us, a five-minute drive at most. The other was with a company called ZAP Paintball, and this was a helpdesk position. After a month, I was losing hope that either of those companies would call me back and I started to wonder if I would ever break into the field of IT again.

I still hoped upon hope that NOVA would call me. I finally received a call one Friday afternoon from ZAP Paintball, asking if I would still like the position, as they were prepared to offer it to me. I asked for the weekend to consider it while secretly hoping NOVA would call me Monday morning. Monday came and went and finally I had to admit that NOVA wouldn't be calling. I called ZAP Paintball back at 2:00 p.m. on Monday and said that I would love to accept the position. A little after 3:00 p.m. that same day, NOVA called to offer me the job. I was disappointed, but I felt as though that must have happened for a reason. I declined, as I had just accepted another offer. I sent each of my NOVA interviewers a letter thanking them for the interview, and ultimately the job offer, expressing how disappointed I was in the way it had worked out. I wished them well in their search and said that I hoped we would end up working together one day.

Over the years, Clarence and I got more involved at church. One of the men in our small group served as the youth pastor. One night we were supposed to have small group, but nobody could make it and it ended up just being Aaron (the youth pastor), his wife Lydia, Clarence, and me. We sat around a fire as Aaron and Lydia started talking to me about becoming a youth leader at the church. They thought I would enjoy the teens and that the teens would like me as well.

This was great timing because I'd been missing volunteer work since leaving my job in London, and hence my volunteer position with the Distress Centre in London as well. I had considered becoming a Big Sister, but wasn't sure if that was the best fit for me. I wasn't sure I would be a good leader to teens, but Aaron told me to just come out one or two nights to see what I thought. Then I could decide for myself.

I showed up and discovered that I actually have quite a bit in common with teenagers. For starters, I'm often confused and think that I still am one. Secondly, I love the way teens communicate. They haven't fully entered into the world of adulthood where people monitor what they say and try hard to project a certain image. Teens are much more real than that and have an easier time speaking their minds. I found being around them refreshing, and occasionally one would even ask me for advice! This was something I took very seriously, as I would never want to lead a teen (or anyone else, for that matter) astray.

I found myself praying more and asking for guidance to help me deal with issues as they arose. Amazingly, I felt as though God was answering those prayers and He often helped me find the right words. I remember telling one teen while at a retreat to just go out on a limb and ask God for a sign—any sign, big or small—that He was with her and that He knew her heart and was taking care of her. We prayed about this, and then she said, "Thanks." She walked away looking dejected, as though she didn't really expect anything to happen. In that moment, the band started to play a song she hadn't heard for a long time. It was a song that she loved; she felt it had gotten her through some tough times, but she hadn't heard it in ages.

She ran up to me. "Nobody but God and I know what that song means to me," she said excitedly. "What are the odds they would play that exact song right now?"

I marvelled at how God can work in such small but obvious ways and was left feeling in awe of Him for about the thousandth time.

Aaron and Lydia eventually decided to move out west where Aaron could return to school and upgrade his education. Lydia quickly found a nursing position there as well. Our small group was saddened to become a little bit smaller. H20 (the name of the church's teen group) suffered for a while, but a new youth pastor was found; life moved forward for everyone.

ZAP Paintball was a permanent full-time position and I was ultimately glad I had taken it. I met Leslie there, and we became instant friends. Then there was Sarah in Human Resources, who was the same age as us and lots of fun, and Brad (Be-Rad), who made me smile every time I saw him. He reminded me of a young Clarence with his great work ethic and sunny personality. And I also met John, who taught me so much. The work was relatively easy, we rarely saw our boss (which gave us lots of freedom to do our work as we saw fit), and everyone genuinely liked each other. Because this job was in Strathroy, I continued to see my family fairly often. Clarence still loved his work, I was very happy with mine, and once again things seemed almost too good to be true.

One night at H20, Dave, the new youth pastor, showed a video about making time for quiet in our lives, and then we broke off into small groups. I thought I was being brilliant when I suggested to the girls in my group that they should keep a journal for two weeks. During those two weeks, they were to make a point of finding quiet time, then see how life changed for them, or if it did at all.

"Why don't you do that and let us know how it goes?" one of the girls quickly replied.

Trapped! I realized that I was suggesting a lifestyle change for them that I hadn't even attempted for myself, so I agreed that I would do it, and I would let them know how it went. That girl was Amelia, and to this day I owe her a big thank you.

I was astounded at how difficult I initially found it to find quiet time, and then again at what a huge difference it made in my life! I decided that since I had a fifty-minute drive to and from work, I'd use that time. This was difficult because I loved listening to music and I almost found quiet time in the car by myself to be awkward. What I did was listen to the radio station until I drove out of range. Then, instead of finding a different station, I turned the radio off altogether. This left me with about a ten- to fifteen-minute window both to and from work to just sit quietly by myself.

Initially I found the quiet annoying. I quickly realized that it wasn't actually quiet. When they weren't drowned out by the radio, I noticed a lot of thoughts running around in my head. I started to slow them down and try to figure out what those thoughts were, one by one. Some of them were as simple as "I'm hungry," but others were deeper, more intense. They were things that had been bothering me or weighing me down and I tried not to think of, but once I cleared away the noise I could hear them more clearly. I started to become very in-tune with my thoughts and feelings.

Not only that, but some completely unexpected things happened. I lost weight! It turns out that I ate for all sorts of reasons, but one of them was to suppress feelings that were bothering me. Once I started working through my thoughts, my need to eat sugars and comfort foods lessened. Now that I wasn't eating as much junk food, I started to feel better about myself in general and seemed to have more energy. The list of benefits was actually quite long!

I typed up my daily journal and gave it to Amelia. I think she was surprised that I actually did it. That was a good lesson for both of us. I learned to practice what I preach in order to reap the rewards, and she learned to be careful what you challenge people with; they may just take you up on it.

Then We Were Three, and Other Crazy Developments

Enter Sixx. Clarence and I somehow came to the conclusion one day that while we weren't ready for children, it might be fun to get a dog. Actually, I was content with our two cats. They were low maintenance, cuddly, and life was easy. Clarence got stuck on the idea of a dog, though, and that was that. I said I would only agree to it if we could get a Doberman. My biggest mistake was thinking that just because I had worked with really well-trained Dobermans, I would be able to train a Doberman well. I learned quickly that one has nothing to do with the other.

We were both big *Seinfeld* fans and recalled an episode where George said that if he ever had a daughter, he would name her Six. Everyone thought he was crazy, but then one couple had a baby and named their daughter Six and he was devastated that his original name had been stolen. We thought it was funny and used that as our inspiration to name Sixx, spelled with two x's to change it up a bit. What we failed to remember correctly was that on *Seinfeld*, it was *Seven* that George said he would name his daughter. Maybe that was our first sign that we had no business getting a dog. We couldn't even get his name right!

This little pup was so tiny and cute, but his massive paws gave us a hint as to the size he was going to be and I don't know that I had really thought through what it would be like to have a small horse running around the house. Sixx immediately decided that he was dominant over me, and no matter what I did, nothing seemed to change that. I had zero control over this dog, even as a pup. Clarence had more, but he still challenged us over every little thing.

Our marriage got knocked around a bit as this dog tested us in every way. We couldn't even correct him with a leash or by spanking, because he was so strong everything seemed like a game to him. If I spanked him, he would act as though I was petting him, so my attempt at disciplining him turned into praising him for bad behaviour. If I jerked the leash to correct him, it barely caused him to move. We were in over our heads and knew it, but we were both so incredibly stubborn. Neither of us was willing to admit defeat.

We found ourselves waking up each morning giving each other pep talks: "Today is a new day. We will be better at this today." We tried to get him running outside as much as possible to burn energy, but no matter how long we had him outside, it never seemed to be enough. We would take him to fields to let him run and to dog parks where he could play with other dogs, but he always wanted more. Eventually we got used to this new life of ours and found ways to adjust.

Some of the guys in our small group planned to attend a Promise Keepers event that year, a men-only event. There were to be hundreds of men of all ages in attendance, all of them seeking to know Christ or looking for a renewal of their faith, as sometimes our faith can be put on the backburner for too long and become stale. Clarence had to work that weekend so he didn't go, but it didn't matter; we were changed just from hearing the stories the men came back with. They were excited because a friend of theirs, Jeff, had suddenly "got it." He felt called by God and began to see what it all meant. His newfound fire for God was inspiring to all of them.

One of the speakers that year was especially intriguing, and one man bought a tape of his presentation. He left it with Clarence and me to watch; it excited me and left me wanting to test his theories. He spoke about being generous with our time, money, and talents, but he focused on money. The reason he did this was because he himself had experienced some crazy things in his walk with God. Numerous times in his life he had been asked by God to part with things he owned. Each time he struggled with it but did as God asked, and each time God blessed him with something even better than what he had given up.

After hearing example after example, I decided that I wanted to know God in this way. I knew He was capable of forgiving me and helping me through tough times, but I had never really considered giving my money to him. Quite the contrary; I was focussed on getting better jobs that paid more money. I wanted to have a good title and a large salary by a certain age—that was how I thought I would know I had "made it" in life. This man taught something very different. He suggested that if you actually gave your things to God and agreed to obey Him and direct your finances (and anything else He required of you), you would find yourself wanting for nothing.

Clarence and I had gotten some advice from a coworker of his when we first got married. He suggested that the person who was less capable of saving money should be the person to pay all the bills. That would force this person to put their money toward things that were necessary and important, freeing up the other person's money so they could save and invest it. We thought that was smart advice. Since I was much more likely to spend impulsively, I took on the task of paying our bills. By the time the bills were paid, the car was filled with gas, and groceries were bought, I had no money left. Not a dime.

Clarence, who made much more than I did, started putting all of his money into savings and investments. He also paid for the trips we took. For the most part, this worked well for us, but there were times when I felt bitter that I couldn't even buy a shirt without having to ask for money from his account.

This bothered me, since I worked hard as well. I felt as though I had no financial freedom. However, the speaker from Promise Keepers was talking about giving all your money to someone else, but experiencing complete financial freedom at the same time. I was sold. I decided that I wanted to tithe my money by giving ten percent to the church. The problem was that I rarely had money left over to give. (I didn't completely understand tithing yet, since it actually means to give the *first* ten percent, not whatever is left over). That didn't prevent me from giving ten percent, though. Each week I had to ask Clarence to help me so that I could give the right amount. I know this seems odd, but I wanted to give ten percent of my income, even if it meant borrowing from my husband's account to do that.

I can't say that I suddenly won a lottery or money rained out of the sky into our backyard. I just started to feel very good about it.

Parting with money became easy and felt like the right thing to do. The more I looked forward to tithing, the more it became important to me. My priorities began to change when it came to spending money.

We seemed to do well financially and definitely felt taken care of. I wanted Clarence to start tithing as well so that he could experience this same feeling. We talked about it a little, but he was so intense about saving that this was a harder concept for him than it was for me; I was already used to feeling broke. He said he wasn't against it at all, but he always forgot to write a cheque and never had cash on him. "If they would offer a debit machine, then I would give," he once said. This excuse seemed very lame to me, but I stopped bothering him about it and continued to give on my own and pray about Clarence. He had always seemed much steadier in his faith than I was, but for the first time I felt as though he was lagging behind. That frustrated me. Men were created to be leaders and I didn't want to tell him what to do; I wanted him to know what was right and lead us accordingly. This became a focus of my prayer.

Life moved on and things continued to get better and better. In December 2005, Clarence and I booked a vacation over Christmas and New Year's. We spent a week in Cuba at a Sandals resort. Of all the trips we took together, this one was by far the best. The resort was beautiful, the food was indescribable, and the entertainment was fantastic every single evening. We felt as though we were living in a dream all week long. The weather was perfect and we were able to completely relax by the pool for days at a time, reading and chatting.

Things would change for us immediately upon returning home. It was a cold, nasty January and both of us started to feel sick. We figured we had likely picked up a flu bug of some sort on the flight. I had a sore throat, sore ears, and felt awful in general. Clarence complained of discomfort in his chest, difficulty breathing, and the occasional shooting pain that would hit anywhere from his left shoulder to his chest or back. The problem with Clarence and I was that we were "one-uppers." If he mentioned that his throat hurt, I would jump in with, "Mine too! It's been bad for a few days now." If I said my ears hurt, he would follow with, "Yeah, I have this weird pain in my left side." We were so busy one-upping each other that we weren't really hearing the other person.

When February was just a few days away and neither of our symptoms had gotten any better, I suggested that maybe it was time we stopped being so stubborn and made a doctor's appointment.

Because he was a paramedic and I had spent a few years working in a hospital, we were both of the mindset that we would never go to a hospital unless we were critically injured or verging on death. It's fine to not want to abuse the medical system and run to your doctor for every little cough or sniffle, but there's such thing as going too far in the other direction as well.

I finally made the decision for us and made an appointment with my doctor. I then called his family doctor and made an appointment for him as well. We each saw our doctors on the same day. When I returned home that day, I had a bag full of medication.

"Well, she said it looks like the worst case of strep throat she has ever seen," I reported. "Or it could be mono. What about you?"

"He didn't give me anything," Clarence replied bitterly. He listened to my breathing and said it definitely wasn't pneumonia, but he would like me to have some chest X-rays taken, so that's all I had done."

"Looks like one of us had some legitimate complaints." I then teased him about trying to one-up me when I was clearly the one who was more ill.

We went to church and Clarence did something that surprised and impressed me. He turned to me and said, "You know how I've been reluctant to tithe? Well, I realized that I was just making excuses. If I find it too difficult to give each week, I'll just give it all upfront now. I've averaged out what I've been making in the past two years and I think I can accurately guess what I'll make this year, so I've written a cheque for ten percent of that."

It was a cheque for a little over ten thousand dollars.

I was so excited to see my husband back in full form and living his life for God first. I knew that God had answered my prayers and there was no doubt in my mind that he was about to be greatly blessed for his faithfulness. When Clarence put that cheque on the offering plate, I asked him if it hurt.

"I thought it would," he said, "but I can't even tell you how good I feel right now.'

My symptoms cleared up fairly quickly with medication, but Clarence continued to struggle. A few days later, he told me when I got home from work that something crazy had happened to him that day. He had been walking Sixx through a field when he experienced an intense pain on his left side that drove him to his knees. I begged him to go to the emergency department to get things checked out, but he said he was fine and it had passed. He didn't want to go. Ultimately, he was worried that if it turned out to be nothing, he would look ridiculous, especially being a paramedic. I said there was no possible way a pain that could cause you to drop to your knees was nothing, but he held firm and insisted he was fine.

A few days after that, I was at work when I got a call from him. He sounded odd—scared, almost. I asked what was wrong and he said that he was in so much pain that he physically couldn't get out of bed. He had just managed to reach over to the phone to call me.

I said I would call our neighbour to see if she could help him get to the hospital. If not, I would call an ambulance. I didn't want him to wait for me to get home because he would be lying there for nearly an hour. He said he didn't want to do that.

"Why don't you call your family doctor?" I asked. "He may have gotten back the results from your tests. Maybe he'll be able to at least tell you what the problem is. Once you know, it might take away some of the fear."

He agreed to do that and said he would call his doctor, then call me back to let me know how it went.

A few minutes later, my phone rang again. I had never heard him sound so incredibly quiet, small, or scared. He told me in a whisper that when the secretary had answered and he identified himself, she cut him off immediately and said, "Clarence, the doctor needs to speak with you right away."

The doctor was immediately put through to him and said that he had received the results that morning and that Clarence needed to get to a hospital immediately. He couldn't make out exactly what it was, but he thought it could be an aneurysm. I asked Clarence if he was able to get out of bed to get to the hospital or if I should call for help.

"No, I think I can do it," he said. "I'll drive myself there."

"Okay," I replied. "Be careful please. Call me from the hospital and let me know once you know what's going on."

He quietly said, "Okay."

We hung up.

I sat there for a solid minute in shock before I realized what I had done. Let me know how it goes?! What was *wrong* with me? Wasn't an aneurysm serious? Hadn't people died from aneurysms? I phoned Clarence back as quickly as my shaking hands would allow and he answered right away, almost as though he had been waiting for me to call back.

"I'm so sorry, Clarence. Can I meet you there?"

"Yes please," he said in the most terrified voice I had ever heard come out of his mouth.

That was all I needed. I told him to get there as quickly as he could and I would be there.

I flew out of the building, ran to the car, drove 140 kilometres per hour all the way there, parked, and was in the emergency department in about twenty minutes. The whole way there, I was thinking, *I will stop for no one and I will run over anyone who gets in my way.* More importantly, I was saying "Please God. Please God. Please God" without ceasing.

"Please let him be okay. Please let him be alive when I get there. Please give me a chance to say how much I love him. Please don't let him die alone. Please heal him. Please. Please."

Pleas and Prayers

His doctor faxed over the test results. The hospital wasn't sure what they were seeing, so they ran tests of their own. Clarence was pale and frightened. He had been coughing for most of January, but the doctors asked him to be as still as he could. If this was an aneurysm, they didn't want him to do anything that might cause it to burst. Do you know how difficult it is to not cough when that's all your body wants to do? He held his coughs back, though, which made him crazy, but he was frightened enough to do it anyway.

We were in Sarnia Hospital for more than six hours while they tried to figure out what they were dealing with. At one point, I stepped out into the hallway and I saw some X-rays hanging up on a screen that said "Lenting" in the bottom corner. I'm not a doctor and I don't know how to read x-rays, but I knew it was bad. I went into his room and told him I had seen his results hanging up. He asked me what I'd seen.

"Do you want to hear this?" I asked.

He said he did.

"Clarence, it isn't good. There's a huge dark spot on your X-ray. I don't know what it is, but something is very wrong."

The doctor finally came into the room to tell us that they didn't know conclusively what they were dealing with, but it was one of two things—either an extremely overactive thyroid or one of a few types of cancer.

Come on, thyroid!

We left the hospital with this knowledge and were told that we would receive a call shortly with more information. Exhausted and starving, we walked to the car in a daze, then decided we needed to eat, and quickly. We silently prayed that this was nothing more than a thyroid issue, all the while knowing deep down that this wasn't going to be the answer. Somehow when you're told that it could be one of three different types of cancer, or a thyroid issue, you just know it isn't a thyroid issue.

Clarence got a call the next day and the doctor said that they believed it to be a cancer of some sort, but they weren't sure which type. Until they knew this, they wouldn't know the best way to treat it. He had two options: they could either use a needle to get a small sample to try to determine the type (but the odds of getting a conclusive answer weren't great) or they could perform a surgery in which they'd open his chest and take a large sample, thereby getting a conclusive answer. The first option was much less invasive, but answers would be slow in coming and he could end up needing the surgery anyway. Clarence didn't know what to do and said he would call them back. He then called me at work and asked what I thought. The catch was that they wanted an answer that day because they could squeeze him in for surgery within a day or two if they knew the answer immediately.

This felt like a lot of pressure and I certainly didn't want to give the wrong answer. What if it wasn't a cancer and we had his chest opened up for nothing? On the other hand, what if it was and we missed it by not acting fast enough? This was a massive decision and I couldn't bear to be the one making it. We were both at a loss and felt frantic over it.

I suggested that we contact my sister and her husband Rob, who were both doctors, to see if they could help us come to the right answer. I called my mom and explained the situation. She was heartsick to hear what was happening. She gave me my sister's cell number and I called her while at work. She wasn't sure and suggested that her husband might be the better one to ask. She had me call him, and while I did that, she spoke with her coworkers to get their opinions.

I called Rob and explained the situation. He laid out the pros and cons of each, but didn't tell me which way to go. I thanked him and hung up, still not sure what to do. A couple of minutes later, my phone rang and it was Rob calling me back. He said that Clarence had to have the surgery. He sounded a little frantic himself and told me that if it was my sister, his wife, and he had to make a decision like this, he wouldn't want to waste any time getting the proper treatment for her. He knew in his heart that surgery was the way to go.

That made sense to me.

I always liked Rob and considered him to be a great brother-in-law, but in that moment he became my brother. I trusted his judgement implicitly and called Clarence back to share what everyone had said. Clarence signed up to have surgery.

I had been on a fairly gentle walk with God up until this point in my life. I had made bad decisions along the way and gotten a little battered and bruised here and there, but I felt as though He always helped me out of those situations. I didn't always know it at the time, but I could look back and see how He had woven things together in my life to work for the good. I felt as though my faith was strong and I loved and trusted God, but I had never experienced this kind of need for Him before. My faith was changing daily as Clarence and I waited for appointments, then results, and then figured out how to deal with each thing that was thrown at us along the way. My prayer life became intense and filled with desperation.

The surgery went well, and by well I mean that he lived through it. I waited anxiously in the waiting room the whole time, and when they finally rolled him past me, I ran over to him. He looked at me just long enough to say in a bitter voice, "They put in a chest tube."

This was painful and he wasn't happy about it at all. I didn't care. The surgery was over and he was alive and anything beyond that wasn't important.

Waiting for the results seemed to take an eternity and the not knowing was incredibly difficult. When we finally heard back, I realized just how true the statement "ignorance is bliss" really is. Clarence had Non-Hodgkin's Lymphoma.

Cancer.

That big spot on his X-ray was a tumour the size of a one-litre milk carton. It was so large that it had completely pushed his left lung down, leaving him to work with just one lung. That explained his difficulty breathing and pain when he moved certain ways. They said that because he was a young, otherwise healthy male, he had a seventy percent chance of beating this. I remember a time when I would have thought that seventy percent was good, but I found myself thinking that this number wasn't nearly high enough.

It was time to start attacking this tumour and there was no time to waste. He was quickly scheduled to meet with doctors at the cancer clinic in London to begin chemotherapy treatments. They were going to treat him once every three weeks. The hope was that his white blood cell count would have a chance to increase enough within that three-week span that he could handle another chemo treatment, and they would keep on with this treatment plan until the tumour was small or, better still, gone. Then they'd go after it with radiation.

He had to lie in bed for a full day receiving chemo, and fortunately my boss at ZAP Paintball was very understanding. He let me take these days off so that I could be with Clarence. I sat in a chair beside his bed while he slept. Often I bent over so that I could rest my head on the edge of the bed, sleeping with him.

The stress of not knowing what was going to happen next was incredibly draining and we became chronically tired. After his first treatment, we went to the car and realized that neither of us had eaten all day. We were both very hungry and went across the road to Swiss Chalet. The food was good and we ate it so fast we barely tasted it, but within a few hours he was sick from the chemo and threw up in the washroom. Because we had eaten there and he'd gotten sick so shortly afterwards, he forever associated this restaurant with feeling ill. Just driving by it would nearly cause him to heave. I joked that I should have chemo myself and binge on chocolate and ice cream afterward; it could solve a lot of my eating issues.

Clarence and I joked a lot about cancer, being sick, and dying. We had to. If you can't laugh about it, it will destroy you. One thing we had joked about for many years was our marriage. Whenever anyone asked how long we had been married, we would tell them and then follow it up with, "But we'll see how it goes after our ten-year anniversary." If they asked what that meant, Clarence would say with a very straight face that we had agreed to re-evaluate our marriage at the ten-year mark. If things weren't going great, we'd pack it in and call it a day. No hard feelings, no fighting, just split everything evenly and head our own way. Of course, I would have to take the dog, he would say. He'd say all of this with such a straight face that people gave us the strangest looks. Obviously they didn't know us well, because we were clearly a couple that was going to grow old gracefully together and sit on the porch of our cottage one day, enjoying old age and reminiscing about our lives together. When he was diagnosed, we had been married just shy of nine years. I told him that was a copout and if he wanted to leave me, he'd have to pack his bags and do it like a man... none of this "I'm too sick to stay with you" garbage.

His white blood cell count wasn't picking up quickly enough after his first chemo treatment so the doctors wouldn't proceed with the second. They put him on a medication that cost $1500 each time he had to take it, and it was supposed to help with this. It worked, so after each treatment he would have a needle with this medication. Then, three weeks later, he was able to have chemotherapy again. He always got nauseous and would be sick for three days after having received chemo, but on the fourth day he would recover nicely and then have two straight weeks of looking and feeling good.

He really looked better after each treatment and we were confident he was beating this tumour. Since he was on short-term, and then long-term disability while being treated, he was home all day and bored out of his mind while I was at work. He would take Sixx to a park and let him run free while Clarence slowly walked along the path. He got lots of sun, had some good colour in his cheeks, ate well, and put on some healthy weight.

It was therefore shocking when each time the doctors took more tests to see how the tumour was reacting, they would come back looking confused and say, "It isn't shrinking." It would shrink initially, but was so aggressive that it would grow right back. They just couldn't seem to hit it with enough chemo. They admitted him into the hospital where he would receive chemotherapy for three days straight. Again, the tumour made a quick recovery and bounced back.

Between all these treatments, we experienced some pretty amazing things.

A group of doctors, nurses, paramedics, and fire-fighters held a golf tournament and silent auction to raise money for us. Apparently a doctor won a signed jersey in the auction. He put the jersey back in the auction and allowed bidding to continue. The next person who won it did the same, and then it happened again. I'm not sure how many times that happened, but Clarence was so humbled by these incredible acts of friendship and generosity that it brought him to tears.

Next, the 911 hockey league in Sarnia held a meat-raffle to raise money for us. The crazy thing is, we never knew about these things. We didn't ask for them, we weren't a part of the planning, and it was a complete surprise when a friend of ours from our small group came to our door one night and explained what they had done, then shoved over eight hundred dollars into our hands and left.

It wasn't about the money. It was never about the money for us. We had been saving our money for years and he had a great benefit plan that covered the cost of the drugs he was taking. He was even making more money on long-term disability than I was making at my full-time job! Financially, we were fine. It was about people not knowing what to do, but desperately wanting to do something—anything—to see him better. It was about knowing that friends, coworkers, and even random people were willing to do whatever it took to help. It was about God, who knew that we were faithful in giving Him our first, making sure that our minds were put at ease by letting us know that financially we were taken care of.

Parking at the hospital was expensive, and driving back and forth every day for radiation had us filling the car with gas often, so we did use some of the cash toward that. We agreed that when he was through this, we would take that money and find someone else who was in need. We'd share it with them so that this great gift we had been given didn't end with us.

One day I was driving to work when I realized I hadn't turned the radio off for some purposeful quiet time in many months. I decided I should do that again—and this would prove to be an important move. I drove in silence for a while and worked to calm the noise in my head.

As I slowly quieted one thought after another, I realized that there was one continuous thought repeating itself in my brain. It was constant, and it was this: "Please God. Please God. Please God. Please God. Please God." I started to understand why I was starting to feel so incredibly run down and tired. Anyone who has ever loved someone through cancer (or any illness, for that matter) knows that it's a stressful time. I would go to sleep with my hands on Clarence's back and pray for God to save him. I would even ask God to move the tumour from Clarence's body to mine. This may sound like a noble request, but I had a selfish motivation; I was certain that having cancer would be far easier than watching Clarence have to deal with it. The helplessness and worry begin to chip away at you until you end up feeling as though you're a pile of broken pieces on the floor.

I often woke up with "Please God" being the first thought on my mind, but I'd had no idea that this was playing like a broken record in my mind day and night. This underlying panic sapped every last ounce of my energy.

While driving, I did something very important—I turned that voice off. I knew God knew my heart, and Clarence's, and the hearts of everyone who prayed for us constantly. Repeating "Please God" 24/7 demonstrated a lack of faith on my part. I prayed that God would continue to know our hearts and our minds, that He would never leave or forsake us… and then I gave that to Him and stopped carrying it around on my shoulders.

Something else became clear to me as I reintroduced quiet time into my life. I needed to quit my job. I wasn't exactly sure why, since my boss had been great through all this and I adored my coworkers. At first it was just a feeling, but as each day passed the need to quit became almost urgent. I ran it by Clarence and he said that he loved me and knew that we were being taken care of, so if I felt led to quit, he would support that decision.

A few days later, my coworker told me that she'd heard NOVA was hiring again. It was only a six-month contract, though, so she had no interest in it. I called the agency that did the hiring for large companies in the area and told them I had applied for jobs through them once before and I wanted to submit an updated resume for them to consider for the NOVA posting. They accepted it and passed it along.

The next day, my boss came down from Windsor to check on things and I decided to let him know that I was leaving. I knew it seemed crazy for me to leave my job, especially without another one waiting, but my instinct to quit was so intense that I could barely stand it anymore.

That morning, I got a call at work from the placement agency. The girl sounded excited and said, "They remembered you from your interview the last time around and said they don't need to interview you again. They would like to offer you the position. Can you start next week?"

I can't even explain the mix of emotions I felt, but that was the second time in my life God had prompted me to move and as soon as I followed His direction, it was made clear to me why. My job at NOVA paid much more and was just minutes from our house. Now if Clarence called with any symptoms or needed help in any way, I could actually be there for him. This was a huge blessing to us and took a bit of weight off our shoulders.

Clarence was told that if he ever developed a fever, he should go to the hospital immediately until they could get it under control. As his immune system was greatly weakened, even a slight fever was dangerous. This occurred once. That evening, we went to the emergency department and explained his situation. They hospitalized him immediately. I would spend as much time with him as I could, but I also had to make the time to walk Sixx, because if he didn't get out every day for at least an hour he would become unbearable to live with.

When Light Chases Darkness…
Where Does it Flee?

One Saturday morning I got up to take Sixx for a lengthy walk before going to the hospital. Truth be told, I enjoyed these walks because I would have intense conversations with God and it really felt as though He was gently leading me through all this. This particular Saturday, I experienced something so bizarre and so unlike anything I had ever even thought possible that it would change my faith forever.

I did something differently this time. Instead of walking and chatting with God, I started talking out loud to Satan. That's not necessarily something I would recommend, but on this day it just felt right. As much as Clarence and I were both very aware of God's presence in our lives, every time he got negative test results we'd feel as though the rug had been pulled from under us… and it felt as though Satan was doing the pulling. We began to feel like a struggle was taking place in our lives between God and Satan and we were just along for the ride.

For that reason, I decided to have a little chat with Satan.

Had anyone driven by me walking Sixx that day, they would have thought I was completely crazy. I talked up a storm… to nobody. I began to tell Satan that he wasn't fooling anyone. He wasn't being clever and he wasn't as sneaky as he thought. I let him know that we could very clearly see what he was doing and it wasn't working. I told him what a complete coward he was.

It may be easy to mistakenly believe that God isn't with us at times—when things aren't going our way—but one thing God never does is hide in the shadows. He is open and honest and very present to anyone who seeks Him. Satan, on the other hand, is weak and a weasel. He relies on trickery and preys on our every weakness. I assured him that he couldn't have Clarence, because I knew for a fact that Clarence was resting firmly in the palm of God's hand. I also let him know that I may have been tired and worn down, but he was confused if he thought for half a second that this meant I was fair game or an easy target. My allegiance was to God and there was nothing he could do to change that. I then told him that I would never fear someone who was too afraid to even come out of the shadows. I dared him to reveal himself to me, because if he was looking for a fight, I was ready.

This is where the story gets really weird. Just then, I walked under a tree and every single leaf on that tree began to shake. I don't mean there was a breeze and the leaves started to get blown around. I mean, each individual leaf began to shiver and shake. At the same time, two massive black crows seemed to come out of nowhere and swoop low, almost as though they wanted to make sure I noticed them. Sixx saw them at the same time I did and took off like a flash. That dog could run like the wind! He chased those two birds in a giant circle all the way around the park, then out of it. I watched this happen, then looked up to see the leaves still shaking. Then they dropped off the tree—all of them.

I began to laugh hysterically. I could barely contain myself. "That's it, Satan? *That's* what you've got for me? You are truly pathetic. You need to find someone else to toy with because your act isn't working with us here."

I can honestly say I felt as though I'd seen this game of light and dark taking place, and light won. If Satan thought he was going to scare me into submission with some shaky leaves and a couple of birds, he really didn't know who he was dealing with.

Not that I thought I was so tough. Make no mistake, if I had to rely on my own strength to get through my days, I would never have made it out of the house. I would have been a broken heap on the floor and there would have been nobody patient enough to put that many broken pieces back together again. No, this strength came from God and I knew it. It was the same strength that kept Clarence smiling throughout his illness. It was the same strength that allowed me to quit a job at the worst possible time without another job waiting for me. It was the same strength that was going to see us through.

I went to the hospital after that, but I didn't tell Clarence what had happened. It was so bizarre that I wanted to wait a day or two to make sure I still remembered things the same and it wasn't just some crazy dream.

The next day, I woke up and remembered what had happened. I knew that it was real. I wasn't crazy. I hadn't made it up. It was then that I shared it with Clarence, and he was a little taken aback by it all. We were both hyper aware that there was some seriously intense spiritual warfare going on in our lives, but we both felt very much safe and protected in God's arms.

About a week or so later, I came home from work to see Clarence sitting in the living room crying. He never cried. At least, he never cried around me. I knew he cried privately and had some very real talks with God about what was happening, wondering how he would get through it all and who would take care of his wife if he didn't. I was nervous because for him to let me see him cry, he had to have gotten some seriously bad news. I asked what was wrong.

"Our dog has cancer," he said bitterly.

What?

Sixx had some lumps on his skin that at first we wrote off as dog acne or a skin irritation of some sort. At first we only saw one or two, but within a matter of days he had ten or more. A day or two after that, they began to grow in size and were soon the size of a quarter or larger. Clarence took Sixx to the veterinary clinic to see what these strange lumps were and the vet tested one, determining that it was cutaneous histiocytosis.

Cancer.

Clarence wept bitterly. "It's not enough that I've got cancer, the dog has to have it too?"

I knew that Satan hadn't stopped at a few shaky leaves and a couple of crows. It was on. I told Clarence to look at me. "This is not yours," I said. "This one is mine. You need to focus on yourself and take good care of yourself. I will deal with Sixx."

We put Sixx on medication that the vet recommended. It was awful. The medication made him so incredibly thirsty that he would nearly empty our toilet of water. It also made him so lethargic that, aside from getting up to drink, he would lie down and sleep night and day. He would pee in his sleep and we started having to carry this 110-pound dog out to the backyard to relieve himself because he didn't have the energy to walk. This was no life for a dog and Clarence didn't have the strength to carry him outside throughout the day.

I began calling different specialists. I located one in Guelph who worked toward healing animals naturally rather than with medication. I loaded Sixx into the car and off we went. They recommended a few different things and, after dropping a few hundred dollars, we headed home again. He seemed to do a little better with these natural treatments and we began to wean him off the medication. We contacted our breeder to see if any of his other dogs had been known to have this, and they hadn't. In fact, we looked it up online and learned that the Burmese Mountain Dog could be prone to this, but beyond that, if your dog gets it, that's just incredibly bad luck.

Luck had nothing to do with it and there was nothing random about this. I may not have known much, but I knew that. Our breeder suggested we put Sixx on a raw food diet immediately and stop giving him the medication altogether. We tried this and Sixx bounced back in no time. There were spots missing in his fur where the lumps had been, but he had more energy and character than when he had started! I felt as though Satan had failed in this attack, but I was now very aware that he would stop at nothing, using anyone or anything to get to us.

Sometimes the Answer to Prayer is No

Near the end of the year, the doctors decided that it was time to go at Clarence's tumour with radiation. Again, Clarence did so well with this that he was even driving himself to and from radiation some days.

One thing which may seem weird is that we took pictures of Clarence before and after his surgery. He had to shave his chest to have it, so we took pictures of him before in a pair of shorts and without a shirt and then again after shaving his chest. Then we took his picture again when he got home from surgery and had stitches across his body. I would take one last picture of him once the stitches had healed nicely, then take my roll of film to be developed (this was just before having a digital camera was a must). When we got the pictures back, we were shocked at what we saw.

I had forgotten all about them, but our vacation pictures were on this roll of film as well. We had felt so good while in Cuba that we'd assumed we looked fine while we were there, but this wasn't the case at all. We nearly gasped when we saw Clarence in those pictures. He *looked* as though he had cancer! How had nobody pointed out to us how thin and sickly he looked? I suppose when you see people often enough, the change is gradual.

Seeing these pictures was a reality check. Clarence was in a fight for his life. What gave us hope was that in the last pictures I had taken, he had put on weight, gained colour, and looked healthier than he had looked in a long time. If pictures really do tell a thousand words, we prayed that they were telling us he was healing nicely and going to be just fine.

After a month of radiation, the treatments were complete. Clarence was warned that as a result of the radiation, he could experience some fluid build-up in his lungs and that if he noticed this happening he had to go to the hospital so they could drain the fluid. Christmas and New Year's went by and he didn't feel great, but we weren't sure what the next steps were. He didn't have any more appointments scheduled and we weren't quite sure what to do.

In early January, things went downhill quickly. Clarence's breathing became laboured and he started to experience sharp pains. He often wheezed when he lay down, so he wasn't sleeping well at night and he got more and more uncomfortable with each passing day. We weren't sure what to do. Maybe it was more that we were paralyzed with fear. We waited it out for a few days, hoping it would get better, but it didn't.

I called his family doctor and asked if he could please squeeze Clarence in for a visit. They made room for him the very next day. When the doctor saw Clarence, he looked very discouraged. He asked what was being done treatment-wise and we didn't really know what to tell him. We hadn't heard anything from the cancer clinic and nobody was returning our calls. We did tell him that they had mentioned a potential trial that was going to be run soon; we hoped Clarence could get in on that.

He got on the phone and called the cancer clinic to find out for himself. He finally spoke to one of the doctors who told him that Clarence's treatments were over.

"What about this trial that's coming up?" the family doctor asked. "Can he be a part of that?" And then we heard him say, "Oh, I see. Okay then, thank you."

He hung up the phone and turned to us. "I'm so sorry that I'm the one who has to tell you this, Clarence, but your treatment plan is over." We asked about the trial. "You won't live long enough to be able to be a part of it."

The air was sucked out of the room. I remembered the first time I had seen Clarence's name in the church bulletin under prayer requests—"Clarence Lenting, who is fighting cancer." How surreal it had been to see it in print! Somehow that had made it seem more real.

I had been walking and talking with God for a year over this, and for most of it I had prayed for healing. There came a time, though, when I sensed that I was praying wrong. I began to pray for comfort and understanding instead. I believe that Clarence did, too. I think we had both known for several months that he wasn't going to live much longer, but to hear the words spoken out loud... that made it real.

I try not to swear too often. I don't know why this is, but for some reason swearing seems contagious and one word suddenly becomes a long string of profanities. For this reason, I try not to get started at all. In most circumstances, there are more intelligent ways to get your point across. There are times, though, when the only thing a person can say to adequately express their thoughts is "F—!"

Aside from the fact that Clarence was dying, he was in a great deal of pain. His family doctor asked if the cancer clinic could assist with his pain management and their response was that since they were no longer treating him for cancer, he was not their patient. So, that was it. As long as he was young and healthy and looked as though he had a fighting chance, they would get him in for tests, chemo, and radiation as quickly as possible, but now that he had no hope for survival, they washed their hands of him.

We pleaded with his doctor to help us, as his breathing was becoming so laboured and painful that he was beside himself at this point. He called the Strathroy hospital for us, but they were on "shutdown" from a virus that had been spreading; they couldn't risk taking on new patients. He called the Sarnia Hospital, but they were full and had no place to put him.

To our doctor's credit, he didn't give up. He pushed back. "Listen. This is a paramedic who works in your city. This is one of your own. You need to find a bed for him." They said they'd put him on a bed in the emergency department, or even the hallway, until something became available.

We made the drive in silence, not knowing what to say. When we got there, we were introduced to someone whom I lovingly refer to as one of our angels along the way. His name was Dr. Maddison. He talked to us about what was going on and we begged him to help us. We understood that Clarence was dying, but this pain had to be dealt with and we desperately needed someone to believe that this wasn't just "part of the process of dying."

Dr. Maddison studied Clarence for a moment. "Do I know you? You look familiar."

Clarence said he was a paramedic and Dr. Maddison said something that was music to our ears. "I'll figure out what's going on and do everything I can to help you."

He ran some tests and determined that there was, in fact, fluid building up in Clarence's lungs and body. He said that they were going to put a needle in Clarence's back and drain the fluid. He would feel instant relief.

They drained more than two litres of fluid from him. There was so much that it had started to push his organs all over to one side. His trachea was bent from the fluid pressing on it and his heart and lungs had been squished. When the fluid was drained, Clarence coughed and then took a giant breath. The colour came rushing back into his cheeks. He could breathe without pain and he started to look like his old self almost immediately!

Dr. Maddison didn't speak to us as though we were idiots. He spoke to us like two adults who had brains and opinions, and a right to know what was going on at all times. He hid nothing from us and was very easy to talk to. He told Clarence that he could go home if he wanted, and if the fluid built up again, he would have to return to have it drained—or he could be placed into palliative care. Clarence was terrified of going home and then having to fight to see a doctor again, so he quickly opted to be admitted to palliative care.

That's when my denial kicked in.

I guess I thought that because Clarence *chose* to be in palliative, he didn't really *have* to be there. I guess I thought he would just stay until we knew that the fluid wasn't returning and then we could go back home. I guess I thought that somehow it would all just go away. I guess I wasn't quite ready to accept what Clarence already knew was about to happen.

Clarence was in palliative care for a little over three weeks. I lived in his room with him for the last two. Not only that, but they allowed me to bring Sixx to stay with us so I wouldn't have to constantly drive home to let him outside. Sixx and I shared a cot to sleep on, and there was also a nice reclining chair in the room that I would curl up in to watch TV, passing time while I waited anxiously for Clarence to wake up. I didn't want to miss any of his waking moments.

His waking moments became few and far between as the drugs they gave him to prevent pain kept knocking him out. Sometimes he would wake up and ask me to trade places with him because he was tired of lying down constantly. I would lie in the bed and he would sit in the recliner and watch TV. I always felt guilty when the nurses came in to check on him and found us like that. I was convinced they thought I was kicking him out of bed so I could sleep in it. The nurses were really great there, though.

One day, Dr. Maddison asked Clarence if he had any questions or concerns. Clarence told him that he wasn't worried about dying, but he was worried about how he would die. He didn't want it to be long, drawn-out, and painful. Dr. Maddison sat on the edge of the bed and spoke with Clarence in low tones. I watched from the corner of the room and thought that if I hadn't known them, I would have thought it was a father speaking tenderly with his son. He told Clarence that he wouldn't let him die that way. They would give him enough medication to make sure he felt no pain, and when the time came he would end up falling asleep and never waking up. That put Clarence at ease and he seemed to be at peace.

When Dr. Maddison left, I asked Clarence if there was anything that was left unspoken between us. I knew how much he loved me, and he knew how much I loved him, but beyond that... if he were to fall asleep and never wake up, would there be anything he wanted to say to me first?

"Just represent yourself well," he said.

I told him I would and then waited for him to fall asleep before I started to cry.

Tests were run. The cancer was spreading. Clarence hadn't gone to the washroom in quite a while and, sure enough, the tests showed that his kidneys were failing. The doctor told me that it would be the hardest on me now. Clarence wasn't in pain and he didn't have long, but there was no way to tell how long he did have. He could die in a matter of days, or he could plateau for a while and be in this state for a month or more. I had to brace myself for seeing him like this for a while. I was grateful for any time I could get with him, even though he was sleeping more than ninety-five percent of the time.

One day, the doctor called me into another room to meet with him and a counsellor. He believed I understood the situation, but he was worried that Clarence didn't fully understand what was happening and that he was going to die. I assured him that Clarence had known long before I did; acting as though he was going to beat this and be fine was a hundred percent for my benefit.

Our small group showed up one night to say their goodbyes and pray with us. Clarence then did something he had never done before. He prayed out loud in front of a group of people. I think somehow we all knew this was a huge moment for him. Our small group asked us what they should be praying for. We looked at each other and then I said, "Clarence is miserable like this. Please pray that God either heals him completely or takes him quickly so he doesn't have to suffer in this bed any longer."

Clarence nodded his agreement.

Two days later, a girlfriend came by to visit with me and we went out into the hallway to chat. She gave me some soup and told me that I had to eat something. I hadn't thought about food much while in the hospital. It often wouldn't even occur to me to eat. I promised her I would and she said she'd check back on us later, but she had to get back to work. I had a few bites of soup, but I didn't care about it. I went back into the room to see Clarence trying to crawl over the rail of the bed.

I ran to his bedside and asked what was wrong.

"I'm here, what is it? Are you okay?"

He lay back down, then sat straight up. Once upright, he almost flung himself back onto the bed, gasping as though it hurt. He sat upright again and flung himself back, gasping again. He did this over and over again and I didn't know what to do. I ran to the door, and fortunately a nurse was walking by. I told her to come in immediately because something was wrong.

"Can you give him something to calm him down?" I asked. "What's going on with him?"

She said, "I can't, there wouldn't be enough time for it to take effect."

I realized then that Clarence was literally dying, and his physical body was fighting it. His one last battle before he left. I don't know how many times he sat up and threw himself down, but what happened next was nothing short of amazing. He flung himself back for the last time and then just stopped.

He looked up toward the sky, intensely focused on something. It almost looked as though someone was speaking to him and he was straining to hear. Then he raised his head from the bed and stretched his neck out, leaning toward that thing that captured his attention. I wasn't sure what to say or do, but he seemed to be enthralled with something and I didn't want to interfere with that. I stood watching him and waiting quietly. Then I said, "It's okay, Clarence, you can go there. You are going to be great there, and I'll be okay here, too."

In that moment, and with those last words, he slowly lay back on the bed and closed his eyes. No more fighting, just a quiet surrender and he was gone. I remember looking at the nurse and saying, "He left me." It was half statement, half shock.

I had told Clarence once that if he ever sensed he was going to die and he was able to tell I wasn't there, I wanted him to wait for me if at all possible. I would have never forgiven myself had he died alone, and I believe he was trying to get to me, knowing he was about to go. I believe that his earthly body was created to never die; it was created to walk with God in the Garden of Eden forever, and as a result it fought death because it was never supposed to experience it. I also believe that while his body struggled, his spirit was being spoken to. I believe he had his moment to hear from God, and who knows what one sees and hears during that time? To me, it lasted a matter of minutes, but maybe he was being shown his life and all his sins, and all his faithfulness, and was hearing in those last moments, "Well done, good and faithful servant."

A Time to Celebrate

Seeing Clarence die cemented in my mind that God is real and very present in our lives. He knows us before we're even born, and He's there with us as we take our final breaths. I feel as though I caught a small glimpse of that and saw the peace that comes with knowing Jesus as your Lord and Saviour. I had experienced some crazy things with God, but this one moment acts as a constant reminder that even though we don't always understand why things happen or why good people go through difficult times, it doesn't mean God isn't there.

At the age of thirty-one, I found myself planning a funeral for my husband of ten years. One of the things Clarence had always thought was cool was the bagpipes at funerals and weddings. The funeral director asked if I had any special requests and I said, "Clarence likes the bagpipes." He said that wasn't a problem; he knew people who played and he hired someone for the day. Beyond that, I had to pick a casket and flowers, figure out what to dress Clarence in, etc. The flowers were orange to celebrate his Dutch heritage and the clothes were easy—his favourite cargo pants and hoodie. I had two days to get everything prepared. I found the video we had taken of him skydiving, then put together a PowerPoint presentation that showed pictures of him from birth until present. I painstakingly put it to music that he liked for various reasons. I slept very little in order to make sure it all got done, and done well.

One night when I did get a few hours of sleep, I had a dream in which I told a friend of ours that I had dressed Clarence in his cargo pants and hoodie because I wanted him to look youthful and like himself, since he had always worn these things. In my dream, that friend looked at me for a minute and then said, "Just represent yourself well, Jen."

I woke up in a panic. I called the funeral home and told them I had made a terrible mistake and chose the wrong clothes. They said it wasn't a problem at all, that they could still change his outfit. They said that only the top would show, so if I wanted, I could just have them change the shirt and tie. Clarence wore a new black shirt and tie that he had purchased to attend a friend's wedding a year earlier and it looked very good on him. Sometimes I wonder if he found himself in Heaven looking down at his black shirt and tie, green cargo pants, and sneakers and thought, *Really, Jen? This is how you're sending me to Heaven?*

I had forgotten to specify which song I wanted the bagpipe player to play. I'd been hoping for "Amazing Grace," as it was Clarence's favourite, and also mine. The funeral director approached me and said, "I wasn't sure which song you wanted, so I've asked him to play 'Amazing Grace.' I hope that's alright?" For the hundredth time, I thanked God for taking care of the details.

A girlfriend of mine came up to me at the church just before the funeral was about to begin. She asked if there was anything she could do or anything I needed.

"Actually, there is one thing," I said. "I'm going to speak, but I have no idea what I'm going to say. It needs to honour Clarence, and it needs to honour God. Could you pray about that for me?"

She said she was on it.

When it was my turn to speak, I prayed quickly to God that I would say whatever He wanted me to, but I needed Him to help me with the words. I opened my mouth and what came out was truly beautiful. Really, it was inspired. I don't remember what I said. Over the years, people have said things to me like, "Remember when you said this at the funeral?" and I didn't really, but from those comments I've been able to piece together a good part of it. I believe God was with me that day and the Holy Spirit guided my words. It was a blessing to have the opportunity to speak about all of Clarence's wonderful characteristics, and also God's. I believe they both would have been pleased.

I became a target that day.

What I mean by target is that Satan is *not* God. He's not all-powerful, all-knowing, or almighty. He *has*, however, been around for an incredibly long time. He has intimate knowledge of Heaven, as he spent time there as an angel before becoming prideful and believing that he himself should be the ruler of all. He gathered a group of followers, attempted to overthrow God, and was promptly thrown down to earth, never to return to Heaven again, but to rule over Hell instead.

Can you imagine going to this incredible place unlike any other and then behaving badly, getting kicked out, and being told you'll never be allowed to return? It would be devastating to know there were all sorts of people enjoying that amazing place and you could have had that life, too, but you threw it all away. It would be even more difficult to watch as people that you perceived to be less worthy than yourself were invited in.

Satan can never go back, and the only thing that makes him feel better is making sure nobody else gets invited in, either. It's sort of a "misery loves company" mentality. So, what does Satan do? Whatever he can to make sure we never hear the gospel truth, and if we do, that it doesn't make sense to us. He trips us up as we attempt to walk in faith, and when he sees us starting to fully understand God's love, forgiveness, redemption, and sacrificial offering to us, he works overtime to make sure we become distracted, hurt, angry, confused... anything other than being on fire for God.

Someone who loves and knows God intimately is someone who knows what it is to be joyful. Maybe they aren't always happy, as happiness is fickle and fleeting, but they have a joy so deep that it cannot be stopped. These people begin to exhibit the fruit of the Spirit—love, joy, peace, patience, kindness, goodness, and faithfulness (Galatians 5:22).

That isn't to say such people are all of these things all of the time, but they begin to grow in ways that become very clear and very encouraging to those around them. Someone who's walking closely with Jesus has an inner light that shines brightly when they're by themselves or in a crowd. People are naturally drawn to them because they're good, right, and true. They aren't perfect and they still sin, as we are all sinful by nature, but they're self-aware and make real efforts to conquer their sins by asking God to walk them through these things.

We had been through an incredibly difficult time, but even at its worst, God always found ways to remind us that He was there. He was in charge. He knew the plans He had for us. His ways were not our ways, nor were His thoughts our thoughts. We didn't understand why things were going downhill, but we took comfort in knowing that *God* knew. For some reason, it was all part of His larger plan. We relied heavily on Him for comfort, peace, and understanding.

Once Clarence passed away, people started to say crazy things like "It's okay to be angry with God," "You can scream at God if you want to," or "He'll understand if you hate Him right now." I never understood any of this. Of course I was hurting and of course I didn't understand why such a great person had to die so young, and of course I wished that it would all just go away... but *hate* God? Why would I do that? He was the only one who had walked with us through the entire experience, every moment of every day. He was the only one who truly knew Clarence's heart and mine. He was the only one who knew how to speak to me and bring me comfort. Did these people honestly believe that with cards, emails, flowers, or food, *they* would be able to make me feel better? Was I really supposed to find my comfort in them and tell God off? I couldn't even imagine that.

I drew closer to God and found myself separating from the people around me in little ways. I then stood up in front of a church full of people at Clarence's funeral and told them how amazing God was. I explained that His plans were bigger than just Clarence and me; we are all just a small part of one huge master plan.

Shortly after Clarence had been diagnosed with cancer, we were walking through the mall one day and saw a display for World Vision.

Clarence turned to me. "We have to adopt a child."

I knew what he meant. When your last day comes, you'll want to know that you made a difference in at least one person's life. You'll want to know that you reached out to the poor and comforted the weak. These things suddenly become very important.

It was suddenly very important to Clarence. For that reason, we sponsored a little girl in Mozambique named Florentina. Who knows? Maybe Clarence had to become ill to realize that he wanted to do more in order for this little girl to find a sponsor. Maybe God had great plans for that little girl. Maybe the loss of Clarence's life would lead to great things happening on the other side of the world.

We're all connected in ways we cannot begin to understand, nor should we. If we could truly see the entire plan as God knows it, I'm convinced it would be too overwhelming; we would probably mess it up somehow. I'm thankful to Him that I can't see it all, but every once in a while He allows me to catch little glimpses of plans.

While I obviously missed Clarence like no other, I chose not to focus on that. Rather, I focused on thanking God for taking such great care of him. There was no one on earth I would have handed Clarence over to, especially once he was diagnosed. I almost took on a protective mother-bear posture toward him. I would have done serious damage to anyone who hurt him.

I released my hold on him for God, though—and only God. I could live with knowing Clarence was no longer enjoying a great life with me here, because he was celebrating an even better life with his Father in Heaven.

I felt it was important for those at his funeral to understand these things and not be angry with God or turn away from Him. This was a time to celebrate a beautiful life, a wonderful journey, and an amazing destination.

That's why I became a target. Satan doesn't have the power to wipe out a large number of people at once. He doesn't need to. All he has to do is take one person who's madly in love with Jesus, who's sharing that love and passion with anyone and everyone who will listen, and cause that person to fall... hard.

I knew as I stepped off the stage after the funeral that things were about to change between Satan and me. The stakes had been raised. I wasn't just being faithful to God; I was encouraging others to do the same so they might get to experience the peace and joy He was filling me with.

Satan had to do something with me, and he had to do it quickly.

Where I Stand

I need to be very clear about one thing. Just because you love and trust the Lord God as your saviour, that doesn't mean things will be light and easy for you. If anything, I think it means the opposite. We're never told in the Bible that things will be fun and easy; we're told that we are to pick up our crosses and follow Him. I think of the cross Jesus was forced to carry, which was enormously heavy and burdensome. He did it, though, for the glory of God.

Jesus is the only one who lived, walked among men, died, *and* rose again. People in this world place all their hopes and dreams in thousands of different gods, but Jesus is the only one who conquered death. He's the only one who lives and who's able to actively communicate with us in our lives.

I don't think anyone in the world disagrees with the fact that Jesus lived. Historians, scientists, and religious leaders from every religion will agree the evidence shows that this boy was born in Bethlehem and that He grew up a carpenter. Even other religions agree that Jesus existed and was considered a great man, or a great prophet. The fact that He died on a cross is not disputable since many, many people died in that manner during that time. It all comes down to one thing: did or did He not rise from death? To some, this is a great tale, but that's all it is. To others, this is fact and the basis of their faith. Some people will never decide because they weren't there to witness it for themselves, so they don't know.

Here's the thing. There were people *there* during that time who saw and *still* didn't believe. They couldn't comprehend that this had happened. They didn't want to believe that Jesus was speaking the truth when He said, *"I am the way and the truth and the life. No one comes to the Father except through me"* (John 14:6).

To this day, people find it too difficult to comprehend that a man would allow Himself to be put through all of that for our sins. This man, who claimed to be God, could have stepped off that cross at any point in time, could have destroyed everyone there who was torturing and mocking Him, yet He chose to endure the pain and even prayed for all of us!

"Father, forgive them, for they do not know what they are doing."
(Luke 23:34)

When he had received the drink, Jesus said, "It is finished." With that, he bowed his head and gave up his spirit. (John 19:30)

Jesus *gave up* His spirit, it was not taken from Him. There is nothing we could take from Him. He only ever wanted to give us life, and give it abundantly. He *loves* us. He has forgiven us. He even returned for us.

Somehow each of us holds onto thoughts like these: "I know I'm forgiven, but I've done so many regrettable things. I've managed to sink so low. I'm too ashamed to even admit the things I've done. He couldn't possibly forgive me of all this." Why not? What more does one have to do to display such complete forgiveness? Was dying not enough? Does your sin somehow demand even more than that? These are little lies that Satan and his minions whisper in our ears to bring us down and turn us away from God.

If God can't forgive us, He probably even hates us, so why bother standing in His presence? It would make more sense to hang out with people who understand, wouldn't it? That way, you could drink until it doesn't hurt anymore. Maybe drinking isn't your thing, but cutting seems to help distract you from your pain. Maybe prescription medications helped for a while, but even that wasn't enough and now you have to take it in mass quantities.

Why do we continue to punish ourselves when God very clearly stated, "It is finished"? Is it really easier to chase one bad decision with another than it is to own that one bad decision before God and ask Him to help us recover from it? I understand that asking forgiveness is an incredibly humbling thing... but would we really rather not do that, and instead stuff ourselves with food, material possessions, and people who tell us only what we want to hear rather than the truth? Is that really the better option?

God forgave us because He understood that we really don't know what we do. He knows this, understands it, and forgives us for it. In return, all He asks is that we accept His forgiveness, and then stop hurting ourselves. Just stop. Stop this. Stay still, be quiet, and listen. Let Him tell you what you're doing wrong, and why it's wrong. Let Him show you how to walk away from your hurts intact as opposed to flinging yourself at any quick fix that comes along. Let Him love you as you so desperately crave to be loved. Let Him lead you.

It feels humbling to have someone else lead your life. Initially that can be a difficult decision to make, but I have to say... it's incredibly freeing! It's so much easier to let Him make every major decision for you, knowing that it will be good and your life will be blessed as a result.

Have you done such an amazing job of leading your own life that you can't imagine handing the reins over to someone else? I didn't. If left to my own devices, I would do things like become bulimic, date guys who didn't care about me at all, allow wedges to come between me and my family, drown my sorrow in ice cream and chocolate, become humble one minute and prideful the next, and on and on. I knew that I wasn't the best person to be leading my life and it didn't take a huge leap of faith to invite God in and ask Him to do this for me.

I thought it would be fun to follow Him... but I had no idea how unpredictable my life was about to become.

A New Kind of Lonely

The days following the funeral were a blur. I took two weeks off work. During that time, I tried to figure out where all our bank accounts were and which bills got paid from where. I met with the lawyer to get a copy of our will. I met with our financial advisor to get advice and make sure I was taking care of things properly. I met with the insurance company and picked up a cheque for $350,000. That was to be the most bittersweet money I would ever receive. It should have been exciting to receive that much money. I should have felt wealthy. Mostly I just felt empty, alone, and poor in spirit.

I used that money to pay off our mortgage, pay off the car, and pay off a loan we had taken out for investment purposes. Needless to say, I was doing well in that I no longer had any bills to worry about, but I wasn't left with a massive bank account. I also received a life insurance cheque from Clarence's work. It wasn't nearly so large, but still substantial.

The decisions I'd make in the coming months were slightly skewed. I decided to partially finish the basement of our home. We lived in a ranch-style home and the basement was unfinished. We left it that way because it was more space than two people needed. I had it drywalled and the floors done. I then put large mirrors on the wall, hung a punching bag, pulled out the treadmill and stair-master machines that had been hiding down there, and turned this space into my own personal gym. I also spent $30,000 revamping the backyard. I got a hot tub, large composite deck, and beautiful landscaping... all in an effort to create a dream backyard that anyone would want to hang out in.

Secretly, I hoped that this would draw people over and they would want to spend all kinds of time at my place. It was a $30,000 attempt to avoid loneliness. It failed. People were careful about giving me "space" and then they got caught up in their own lives. Ultimately, I found myself very much alone nearly all the time. The cards and phone calls flooded in for a couple of weeks, but once that ended, it seemed as though everyone had dropped off the face of the earth. It was me and Sixx against the world.

I returned to work, but not really. I didn't care about it. I didn't care about anything. Nothing made sense to me anymore. What was the point of work? To save money, but for what? So I could buy a nice house and a nice car and take some nice trips? I had a nice house and two cars and money in the bank and I didn't care about any of it. I would have given it all for my old life back, if only for a day. I would go to work, put in my time, go home, and eat something quickly while standing over the kitchen counter. Sitting alone at the kitchen table felt odd. Watching television seemed lonely. Funny shows can lose their appeal when there's nobody to laugh at the jokes with. Frightening shows can be awful when there's nobody around to remind you that it's just a show.

The TV didn't get turned on for months after Clarence died. I would eat quickly, then throw a leash on Sixx and head off to one park or another. I preferred places where I could let him run off-leash, so I often took him to the schoolyard late at night. It wouldn't have been uncommon to see us walking around anywhere from 11:00 p.m. until 1:00 or 2:00 a.m.

Sixx was off as well. He was used to having Clarence home every day and now he had to deal with only having me, and only in the evenings. He fell into a slump and I didn't know what to do for him. He still considered himself to be dominant over me and we battled often.

I had gained quite a bit of weight the year Clarence was ill. We felt that spending time together was more important than cooking meals, so we ate out often. While he lost weight, I put it on. I was twenty pounds heavier by the time he passed away. As a result, an old back injury began to cause me some real problems. In my early twenties, I had slipped a disc while working out and every once in a while it resulted in lower back pain. When I gained weight, this pain became constant and sometimes crippling. Sometimes when I attempted to get up from a chair, my lower back would lock and I wouldn't be able to stand up straight. Bent over, I'd have to walk to a bed or couch and lie down. I would then have to curl up in the fetal position and slowly straighten my back and legs. Only then would I be able to stand normally again.

One day I sat in the living room on the chair, just staring into space. I made a move to stand up and, sure enough, my back locked up. I said, "Ow! My back hurts so badly." I felt a little foolish as I realized nobody was around to hear me. What was the point of saying this out loud? I didn't need to tell myself; I already knew I was hurting. I moved to the couch and straightened my back, then got up and moved to the office where I decided to check for emails. As I was at the computer, an incredible wave of sadness came over me and I began to sob. Sob may not be the right word, as it was more like a wail. All this emotion came rushing out of me and then, suddenly, I turned it off. I realized once again that this was foolish. Who was I crying for? There was nobody around to console me and I didn't need to remind myself I was sad. That was the day I stopped crying, stopped verbalizing when things were wrong with me.

I continued to go to work, come home, walk the dog for hours, eat entire containers of ice cream at a time, then feel gross afterward and decide to "work it off" by dancing until three or even four o'clock in the morning, passing out exhausted for a couple of hours, and then starting all over again. This schedule wasn't healthy and I ended up falling asleep at my desk nearly every day. As much as I didn't care about work, it was never my intention to purposely do a bad job or to cause extra work for my coworkers. I felt badly that I gave such little effort, yet I couldn't stop this cycle I had gotten into.

I apologized personally to each of my coworkers and asked them to be patient with me while I figured things out. I assured them that I didn't want to be like this forever. I also went into my boss's office to tell her how brutal I had been at work and to apologize. I explained that I knew my behaviour wasn't right, but I was having a hard time breaking the habit. I let her know that I was aware of what I was doing and I was going to make every effort to do better.

My boss's name was Jo-Ella and she was another angel along my path. She assured me that while I felt I was doing a bad job, my stats actually indicated I was one of the more productive employees. She told me that while she had never met Clarence, she'd heard all the wonderful things I had shared about him at the funeral and she'd been happy not only that I'd had a great husband and marriage, but that I realized I'd had a great husband and marriage. She fully expected me to need time to find my way. She then told me that she was there if I ever needed to talk about anything.

Even though I placed no importance on my job, Jo-Ella made it a safe place. She was supportive and encouraging, treating me the same way she treated everyone—with kindness, understanding, and respect. I'd thought I would never find a manager as great as Melissa from my days at the Royal Bank, but Jo-Ella proved that it was possible to have more than one great manager, and the fact that I had a great manager during this time was nothing short of a Godsend.

Taking a Ride on
the Crazy Train

The next few months were about to get crazy.

When I say things were about to get crazy, I think what I actually mean is that *I* was about to get crazy. One of the hardest things to deal with when someone you're close to dies is other people. To be honest, I don't think there's really anything "right" anyone else can say or do. People dropped off food and flowers and notes, and while that was always appreciated, none of it made me feel any better. People would say, "If you need anything at all, please let me know," and I knew in my heart that they meant it and they would have done anything for me. The problem is, I didn't know up from down. My world had just been tossed around and if I knew what I needed, I would have asked for it.

In hindsight, I wish people would have just done things without asking. For example, I was used to having a husband who took care of everything outside while I took care of the cleaning inside. He did lots of the cooking and either figured out how to fix things when they broke or seemed to know who to call. I had no experience with any of these things and suddenly having to do it all seemed overwhelming. If you know someone who's struggling with something, don't ask what you can do, just be practical and do something. Don't ask if you can mow the lawn, just do it. Don't ask if it's alright if you shovel the driveway, get it done. Knock on the door and say you're going for a walk and you'd like to take their dog with you. It doesn't mean you have to do these things all the time; even once is great. I was fortunate that I had fantastic neighbours who really helped me out a lot. It just felt draining when others asked what I needed.

What I needed was for someone to turn back time. What I needed was for this to be a bad joke. What I needed was to not wake up alone, return from work to an empty house, eat every meal alone, and go to bed alone. What I needed was for people to stop looking at me with these sad, puppy dog eyes. What I needed was for others to stop saying things like, "I know how you must feel," and then proceed to tell me about the time their grandmother passed away. What I needed was for others to stop trying to relate to me by telling me every awful thing they were going through, because it felt as though I was carrying my own burden, and now they were trying to give me theirs as well. What I needed was a therapist. What I needed was to feel sane again. "What do you need?" is a loaded question, so please be careful when asking it.

I was stubborn. Even though others, including my mom, suggested that I might benefit from talking to someone, I was convinced that I was dealing with things very well; I had a Counsellor in Jesus and we talked constantly, so I was fine. Little did I know just how much I was counting on Jesus to "fix"! Thankfully, He has experienced every possible emotion and every sort of pain, and He never failed me. Not once.

I would have benefited from talking to someone, though, because he or she could have told me that some of the things I was thinking weren't true or right. They could have told me that it *is* healthy to cry, even if nobody else is around. They could have told me that it *is* fine to voice your aches and pains out loud, whether someone hears you or not. It's normal to just put these things out there. If I had confided those two things to someone and given them the opportunity to set me straight, that would have helped in all sorts of ways. I was stubborn, though, so it took me much longer to figure these things out.

In March, just two months after Clarence passed away, my mom, dad, and oldest sister took a trip to Texas. I told my mom that I was losing my mind around people in general and she suggested I join them to get away for a bit. When I returned, people would have normal things to ask me about, like "How was the trip?", and it might seem better for me. This turned out to be good advice. It was nice being in a place where I was just known as a tourist and not "that poor young widow." People talked to me with normal

voices and normal expressions. My sister and I took surfing lessons
one afternoon and a few days later I rode a mechanical bull. These
things seemed fun and exciting and acted as wonderful distractions.
My mom was right; the more fun or crazy things I did, the more I
had to talk about with others. I was hooked.

That's when I decided I was going to throw myself into all
sorts of different activities. Not only would I be able to have fun
in the process, but others would again be able to have fun around
me as the conversation naturally steered toward my new hobbies
and adventures. Now was the time. I was single, I could financially
manage, and I was relatively healthy. I had lost a lot of weight in
walking Sixx for so many hours each day. My back still gave me
some problems—it had gotten weak—but it was more bearable now.

We returned from Texas and the very night my parents dropped
me off I decided it was too early to sit at home on a Saturday evening. I showered, changed, and did something I had wanted to do
for a long time. I went to a bar—by myself. I know that seems odd,
but I always found it interesting that guys could walk into a bar by
themselves and not be overly concerned about it. You would never
see a girl walk into a bar alone. Mostly because, who wants to be at
a bar alone? But also, we tend to lack the confidence to do it.

With this new attitude of wanting to do anything and everything, and not caring what others thought, I decided tonight was the
night. I didn't actually drink; I just got a glass of water and hung
out. The night I went, there was live music and the band was really
good. I enjoyed just hanging out quietly by myself and watching
them play. Also, the people-watching was great. It turns out guys
are fairly intrigued by girls who go to a bar by themselves; they'd
watch me for a while, waiting to see if someone was joining me,
then finally come over and say, "Are you here alone?" When I said
I was, we'd end up chatting the night away.

I learned that going out alone wasn't that difficult and usually
ended up in meeting nice people. Sometimes even women would
ask if I was alone; when they heard I was, they would invite me to
hang out with their group. It may sound pathetic, but I started to do
this more often. I only went when there was live music, and never
to get drunk or "find a man." It was never my intention to chase a
bad situation with a bunch of bad decisions.

You may wonder why I didn't go with a girlfriend. Well, I
didn't have many girlfriends; I literally had three. One worked in
youth ministry and couldn't be seen hanging out in a bar, even if
we weren't drinking. The other was married and because I was now

single, her husband assumed I was out trying to pick up men and that I would encourage his wife to do the same. (I love how the minute you become single, you're suddenly prowling for men and have thrown all your values out the window.) She came with me once, but it started to cause fights between her and her husband, so it wasn't worth it. The third, my good friend Michelle, would have absolutely gone with me, but she lived an hour and a half away and I couldn't ask that of her. To be honest, I didn't mind going by myself. I was starting to enjoy spending time alone and figuring out what my likes and dislikes were. This was far better than sitting at home eating a box of ice cream. At least I was meeting people and getting out there.

The next day, I discovered something else: Facebook. One of my friends told me about it and once I signed up I was hooked. This very quickly became the thing I could do while at home to keep me from sitting in front of the TV by myself or eating. I loved that there was always someone online to write a comment on a picture of mine, or write something funny on my wall. I didn't write much on other people's walls, though. I'd write comments on my own wall, people would reply, and then I'd reply to their comments—forcing them to keep coming back to my wall if they wanted to see my reply. I promoted my wall as "the place to be" and before long I had a small group of regulars who kept me company there. It was the online equivalent of what I'd tried to do by building an incredible backyard, but this time it worked. It was as though I had company any time I needed it.

Shovelling snow off the driveway sucked, but mowing the lawn was even worse. The first time I did it, I brought the lawn mower out to the front yard and tried to start it, then tried, and tried, and tried some more. I realized that I wouldn't have to worry about cutting the grass because I wasn't able to start the mower. There I was, standing on the front lawn in the middle of the afternoon—and I lost my mind. I cried, I kicked the lawn mower, and then I sat down and sulked. I channelled every three-year-old tantrum you could imagine.

After exhausting myself, my stubbornness kicked in and I decided there was no way I was going to let this thing beat me, so I tried and tried until finally it roared to life. It was a huge accomplishment for me to get the lawn cut, and it renewed my determination to attack anything I did with a vengeance. I would not be beat. Every time something like this happened, I thanked God for helping me. All these little trials only worked to strengthen our relationship.

One day I drove to Wal-Mart with Sixx in the car. I was going to run in and out, then take him to the dog park. As I pulled into the parking lot, a random thought of Clarence popped into my head and I got very choked up. Then I got angry. "Really, God? Now? I just want to run in and out. I don't have time for this right now." A single tear rolled down my cheek. Just then, Sixx, who had been sleeping peacefully in the backseat, jumped up and kissed that tear off my cheek. It felt as though God had heard my plea and used Sixx to cheer me up. That made me smile and I was able to continue on with my day.

I ended up meeting a girl at the dog park. As we started to chat, we realized that we lived near one another. She and her husband lived just a short walk from my place and their dog and mine played well together. This was great because now Sixx and I could have "doggy play dates" without having to drive all the way to Sarnia to do it! I really enjoyed my talks with her, and I appreciated her husband's humour; they joked that I liked one more than the other, but that was never the case. They were just great people to have in my life. They came into my life at exactly the right time and were one more thing to thank God for.

One day I wrote something on Facebook about being at the end of my rope, or being "done with everything." Something to that effect. It wasn't a cry for help exactly; I was just making a statement. The next day, I went to work and a coworker whom I completely adored said that a bunch of people were meeting at a campground for a bonfire that night. Did I want to join them? Normally I would have said no because I didn't know the other people going and I would have felt out of place. After having gone out on my own a few times, though, I was less insecure about such situations and realized that I enjoyed meeting new people in different ways. Not only that, but it was a Friday and I was dreading going home to do nothing that night. I thanked him for the invitation and said I would take him up on it. He gave me directions. Before leaving, he told me that he'd seen my Facebook status and hoped I was feeling better.

It was then that I knew where the invitation was coming from. I was no longer sure I wanted to go. It was a pity invite. I was torn between desperately not wanting to be home alone on a Friday and not wanting to be the girl everyone looked at and went, "Oooohh-hhh, so that's the girl who lost her husband." I got home from work, changed my clothes, then headed out.

As I was driving, I began to doubt whether I wanted to be there or not. I was already halfway to the mall and could always just go there and shop for a while before returning home. That way I would have done something enjoyable and Friday wouldn't have felt so awful; I could also go to bed early and get Sixx out for a massive walk on Saturday.

I didn't know what to do, so I gave it to God. I asked Him to give me a clear sign, because I wasn't sure if hanging out with these people would be a good thing for me. I even thought this might be an attack of Satan's. If it ended up being an uncomfortable night, I'd go home feeling worse than ever.

I turned on the radio to 88.3, the Christian station, and heard a musician being interviewed. Normally I would have changed the station right away as I hate talking of any sort and generally just want to hear music, but for some strange reason I left it for a few minutes. I don't remember who was being interviewed, but I'll never forget what he said: "To those out there who are listening, there will be times in your life when you're hurting and feel low. You may be feeling alone in the world and incredibly lonely. There may not always be anything you can do about that, but you *can* change whether you're by yourself or not. It's easier for Satan to attack you while alone than when you have surrounded yourself with good people."

God! When I ask for clear direction, you really come through for me!

I decided that while I may not know most of the people who were going to be at the campground, the few I did know from work were really great people. That's where I needed to be. I showed up that night feeling a little awkward, but confident that this was where I should be. The guys instantly introduced me to their wives and I hung out with the women while the men played bocce ball. It turned out that even their wives were great and I struck up Facebook friendships with them for a while—not forever, but long enough that they got me through some rough times. Truthfully, I don't know if they realize how integral they were in my healing process. It's amazing how God places people in our paths for a season and then they somehow blow away like so many leaves, having left you in a better place in the process. That's just one more thing I'm thankful for.

As much as God was working hard to take care of me, lead me, comfort me, and provide for me, there were still times when I completely fell apart. I remember lying down on the bed in the spare room one night because I didn't feel like walking into my bedroom alone for what felt like the millionth night in a row. I began to cry out to God in desperation: "God, I don't understand this life! I don't care about anything in it. There's no purpose for me here; I don't understand why you've left me here alone. Please God, if you love me, and I *know* that you do, then please, *please* don't let me wake up in the morning. I don't want to be here anymore. I want to be there with you." I fell asleep saying this over and over again.

I woke up the next morning with the sun shining brightly through the blinds and streaming across my face. Sixx lay beside me with his head on my stomach, sleeping peacefully. A voice said repeatedly, *"Patience. Faith. Love. Patience. Faith. Love."* It was the kindest and gentlest way anyone has ever told me to settle down. I knew that I had to be patient because things don't run on our time as much as we wish they would; they happen in God's timing. That had to be enough for me.

I knew that I loved and trusted God, but he reminded me to hold onto my faith. My faith in Him and His plans for me, whatever they were, ultimately kept me holding on. When people wonder how on earth they're ever going to get through a rough time in life, that's the easiest and most truthful answer—faith in God. Not faith in ourselves or in what others will do for us, but faith in the One who knew us before we were born and will love us until the day we die. That's quite literally the only thing that will get you through.

I can honestly say that I understand the allure of suicide. Had I not had Jesus walking me through this dark time, I might have given in. Without Him, there is simply no hope. No chance for change or a future. There's just nothing worth living for if you haven't figured out that Jesus is there. Once you realize that Jesus *is* present, life suddenly becomes worth fighting for, if for no other reason than curiosity… you just never know which crazy/cool path He'll lead you down.

Finally, love. I didn't quite get this part of it, but I thought it could mean a few things: He loved me and I loved Him, so maybe my purpose was to simply love others. After all, wasn't that what it said in 1 Corinthians 13:13? *"And now these three remain: faith, hope and love. But the greatest of these is love."* I guess I did have a purpose. I was now very aware of what it was to go through a great loss, a great deal of depression, and a whole lot of change.

Suddenly there were many more people in the world I could relate to than before. I knew how much God loved me through all this, and Jesus walked me through it. Maybe it was time to allow the Holy Spirit to prompt me in new ways. This was a time to be open to loving others through their "stuff" as I had been loved through mine.

On this particular morning, as the sunlight streamed in, I knew for the first time that I would live. I finally knew that I wouldn't die of a broken heart. I knew that God would give me purpose, and knowing Him, I knew it would be great. Things changed for me at this point and I started to get healthy. Not only did I feel better mentally and emotionally, but I wanted to feel better physically. I began jogging and I became thinner than I had been even before Clarence's diagnosis. I still had back issues, but that was about to change—and in a hurry.

I began to swim because my back didn't hurt at all when I was in the water. Plus, it was great exercise. I thought about maybe getting a personal trainer to help me deal with my back specifically. I started to go to bed a little earlier and get up a little easier, although I still had a long way to go. I was still unable to get through an entire workday without closing my eyes, but I slept a little less, which was at least an improvement. I started to care about my work again and take pride in my job. I actually broke out some hedge clippers and cleaned up the landscaping in front of my house so I wouldn't look like a complete sketch-bomb anymore. Sixx even seemed to shake his depression a little. Yes, things were starting to come together.

Then I passed by *him* in the hallway at work.

A Chance Encounter

One day I was walking down the hall at work when I passed a young guy (my age, I thought) who sort of looked familiar, but I had no idea who he was. He was reading notices on the bulletin board. He looked my way, so I smiled and said hi. He did the same in return.

Upon return to my desk, he was gone. I worked at a large company and he could have been anyone and it wouldn't have mattered to me, but for some reason I felt bothered by his presence. I felt as though I recognized him from somewhere, but I knew it wasn't from work and that meant I recognized him from some area of my personal life. I was content to keep my work and personal life separate. The fact that one might be crossing over into the other in some way annoyed me greatly. I brushed it off and decided to let it go. I had worked there for over six months and that was the first time I had seen him, so I probably wouldn't see him again.

The next night I played volleyball with the church league I had joined. Each week we played at a different church. I had Sixx with me in the backseat. He often slept in the car while I did things, after which we'd drive to a park so he could run free for a while.

I got out of the car. As I walked up to the church, I noticed a guy approaching the front steps at the same time. It was *that* guy! Okay, seriously, what was going on here?

I laughed. "Am I stalking you, or are you stalking me?"

He just grinned. "I'm not stalking you."

He went off in one direction while I headed to the gym.

Who *was* this guy? I vaguely remembered him but I couldn't place from where. I had never seen him, but suddenly he had appeared at my work and now at church? I was curious.

A couple of weeks later, I was hanging out with people from my small group when I decided to ask one of the guys if he knew about this person I kept running into. Jeremy was one of those people who just seems to know everybody. I really had nothing to go on, though. I explained to him that I kept running into this guy and it was bothering me because I didn't know who he was.

"Describe him to me," Jeremy said.

Well, he had brownish eyes and light brown, sort of curly hair. He was about my height, thin build. I had run into him at work, then again at church.

"That must be Dawson," Jeremy explained. "He works at NOVA."

I asked why I would just be running into him at work now, after all this time, and we discovered that while I worked at one site, Greg (Greg Dawson, but everyone called him Dawson) worked at another. Perhaps he had been in a meeting at my site the day we passed each other at work. He worked in Human Resources.

I then wondered why I had run into him at church.

"I know he plays the drums in a worship group," Jeremy told me, "so maybe they were practicing that night?"

I found this all very interesting—a good-looking, professional guy who played the drums. To be honest, though, I didn't care about Greg Dawson. I was satisfied with that answer and probably wouldn't have thought about Greg again except that Jeremy went on to say one last thing: "He's getting baptized this Easter."

Something in my brain clicked. This grown man was getting baptized? Why? I was incredibly curious. Adults don't "just get baptized." Children "just get baptized," if their parents make them. This was different. Any adult who got baptized very clearly had an experience of some sort. They had experienced God in their lives in a real way and were eager to share that experience with others by way of a public baptism. This guy had a God story!

For the next few days, I thought of him constantly. I wondered what his story was and how he had gotten to this place in life. I prayed for him and his well-being. Part of me even wanted to attend his church instead of my own on Easter Sunday so that I could hear his testimony, but I decided last minute that it might seem creepy if he saw me there. I didn't want to interfere with his big moment in any way.

The days turned to weeks, then to months, and Greg quickly slipped out of my mind.

I returned to crushing on a guy I had really liked before Greg came along. This other guy hardly knew I was alive—not in a romantic sense, anyway, but we were good friends and he was an amazing person. We wouldn't have worked as a couple, but I sometimes think that my mind decided to be infatuated with him just a few short weeks after Clarence passed away as a defence mechanism. Daydreaming about him kept me from living the hell that had become my own reality. I spent hours thinking about him and convincing myself that I could be happy again if we were a couple.

One day, I received an email from Jeremy and his wife Teresa inviting me, along with many others, to their place for a barbeque and bonfire. It happened to be on a day I was meeting up with Leslie, a girlfriend from ZAP Paintball, and heading to Windsor to visit another friend of ours. I replied that I wouldn't be back in time for the barbeque, but I would show up later for the fire.

Leslie and I made our way to Windsor and chatted nonstop. We hadn't seen each other in a few months and had a lot of catching up to do. I remember gushing about this guy I had a crush on and told her, "I think I've met my future husband. He doesn't know it yet, but it's true." We had a great time in Windsor and then returned home in the early evening. I dropped her off at her car, then proceeded to Jeremy and Teresa's place.

I was confused when I arrived, because there were no cars there. I knew I had the right day, because it was the same day as my trip to Windsor. I decided to just pop in to say hi and then leave. As I walked toward the house, I saw Jeremy in the kitchen window. He noticed me and waved. Then someone looked over his shoulder to see who he was waving at, and I found myself looking at Greg Dawson.

My mind started to spin. What was going on here?

I walked up to the house and Jeremy opened the door. He said that everyone had brought their children to the barbeque, so they had to leave early. I said I wouldn't stay; I didn't want to keep them.

"No, no!" Jeremy insisted. "We still want to hang out. Why don't the four of us hang out in the backyard for a while? Teresa is just putting our children to bed. Do you mind if I go help her? We'll be down in about ten minutes to visit."

Greg and I said that was fine as we wandered into the backyard.

We sat down and started to chat, realizing that we had quite a bit in common. We worked for the same company, lived close to each other in Corunna, shared some mutual friends, and we both loved to laugh. If you were to ask me what I look for most in a guy, I'd say, "A great sense of humour." A guy who can make you laugh is a guy who can help you get through anything.

Greg made me laugh. I was *laughing!* In the past five months I had smiled and chuckled at all sorts of things, but this sound that was coming out of me, I could hardly stand it. This deep, hearty laugh that I didn't even know I had in me came bursting forth over and over again. The way he spoke, his facial expressions, his quick wit... he was killing me! Clarence had always teased me about my laugh because it could be loud and obnoxious—more like a cackle, really. Sometimes when I laughed, Clarence said, "And your little dog, too!"

This laugh, though... this thing Greg was causing me to do... it was the most beautiful sound I had ever heard. Greg Dawson brought my laugh back. By the time Jeremy and Teresa came outside, Greg and I were already in our own little world. I barely even noticed they were there.

As we left that night, Greg said, "So, maybe I'll email you at work sometime?"

"Sure, yeah," I told him.

I got into my car and knew that I would never hear from him again.

It was okay. I didn't care. Greg had shown me that it was possible to fully laugh again and I would be forever grateful to him for that. I hadn't dated in many, many years, but I knew the old "Maybe I'll call you sometime" was the equivalent of saying, "It was fun, have a good life."

I went to work Monday morning in a great mood. Life was really starting to come together for me. I'd had a great weekend with great friends and I was looking forward to finding more things to laugh about.

Later on in the morning, I received an email from Greg Dawson. Wha?! I laughed out loud when I read it. He had emailed a coworker of his to say that he was going to be using the same application as her and asking if she would show him where to find it. She replied, "Jen Lenting in IT got it all set up for me. You'll have to contact her for this."

God, I love *how you work!*

Greg forwarded this message on to me and said, "Well, I guess I was going to email you one way or another."

I helped him set up the programs he needed and then added a quick response to what he had written. He replied to that, I replied again… and a very funny, very intense email relationship was born. I lived to go to work, just so I could read Greg's funny messages to me. We shared little bits and pieces about ourselves over time. The more I learned about him, the more I liked him.

Deciphering his emails would become a little nerve-wracking, though. He would start messages with things like, "Hey girl." What did "Hey girl" mean? Was that a term of endearment? Was that something you would say to any girl you were emailing? Was this a friendship we were building, or was there more going on? I didn't know, and it was making me lose my mind.

For the second time in my life I became crazy, and I blame Greg Dawson for that!

Fun-Crazy or Crazy-Fun?

That summer, I did some exciting things. I booked a trip by myself to New York, I hired a personal trainer to help me strengthen my core and helpfully reduce my back issues, and I swam—all the way across the St. Clair River from Canada to the United States and back. Some friends of mine rowed beside me in a kayak while I made the round trip one hot, sunny afternoon. It was the most amazing time. I became tired fairly quickly and gave up using my own strength and had to lean on God's.

I spent my time in the water praying and thanking Him for everything. I thought fondly of my years with Clarence and thanked God for allowing me to meet and marry such an incredible person. My life was as great as it was because of Clarence's influence, so I thanked God for those years. I thanked Him for great friends and good health. I thanked Him for holding me up when I had neither the desire nor the energy to stand on my own. I thanked Him for knowing me better than I knew myself, and still loving me. I thanked Him for all of it.

I was actually surprised when I neared Canadian soil again, amazed at how quickly the trip had gone. I felt as though I could have praised God forever. Someone told me after the fact that swimming to the U.S. and back wasn't actually legal. Who knew? Now that I'm aware, I won't be doing it again and I don't recommend that anyone else try. In hindsight, it wasn't the brightest idea considering large ships pass through this water often. My actions weren't always governed by logic during this time, though, so I praise God for getting me safely there and back.

My trip to New York was another life-changing event. I like to try activities, foods, etc. that are typical of a place I visit. For example, when I went to Chicago, I refused to leave without having tried a deep-dish pizza. It doesn't have to be some big, expensive event—just something that will act as a fun reminder of that place. I wasn't sure what to do while in New York, and then I thought of the show *Sex and the City* and wondered what Carrie would do. That's when I knew what I wanted to do in New York. I went online and found what I was looking for. I booked my own personal photo shoot! It came complete with a photographer and hair/makeup stylist who provided me with different looks throughout the shoot. I had to bring my own clothes, but they helped me mix and match them, creating different looks. I was so excited I could hardly stand it.

This trip was a big deal for me. While I had taken plenty of trips before, I had never gone by myself. This was the first time I was responsible for every part of it. I had to select and book a hotel and a flight, I had to figure out how to get to the airport and find my boarding gate, I had to get to the hotel from the airport, and I had to decide where and when I was going to eat each day and how I would fill my time. It was all on me.

Just before leaving for New York, I learned that there were going to be two full-time positions opening up in Client Services at NOVA. Three of us were hoping to move into two spots. I knew that we all did good work, but one of them was a shoo-in because he had been there the longest out of the three and was well-liked. That left one position for two of us. I asked Jo-Ella if I could speak with her and told her that I was in a rare position for someone my age. I didn't have car payments or a mortgage, and I had savings to fall back on. I didn't have any children to worry about feeding or clothing, and I was confident I could take care of myself, even if I had nothing more than a good part-time job at a restaurant or grocery store. I told her that if she had to choose between the two of us, she should hire my coworker. That may make me sound as though I was making some great sacrifice, but you have to remember that it really wasn't big of me at all; that's just where I was in life. I would leave for New York in a matter of days and I was fairly confident that I would come home to discover that I no longer had a job.

I told Greg about my trip in an email and he gave me easy directions to the airport (it turns out it's just plain easy to get to).

That was one hurdle out of the way. The day before I was to leave, I realized that I didn't know where my passport was. I was up until 3:00 a.m. looking for it and never did find it. I had to get up and leave by 5:30, so I was working on almost no sleep. At that time, you could drive across the border with just your driver's license. I hoped upon hope that this would be good enough, and good enough for the flight as well.

It was. I arrived just in time to hear our flight being announced and walked right onto the plane. Perfect timing! I was so exhausted that I fell asleep immediately. I woke to the sound of someone snoring loudly. I looked around the plane angrily as I wondered who the chainsaw was, only to realize it had been me! I stopped glaring at the others and snuggled back into my seat.

I was supposed to arrive in New York and take a taxi directly to the flat where my photo shoot was to take place. I arrived right on time, but looked awful. My eyes were heavy and red and I was grateful to have a makeup artist who could help cover that up, at least a little.

I had *so much fun!* I felt like a rock star as I was told to pose this way or that. The photographer turned on a fan to blow my hair around and it was all I could do to not giggle. I left with my photos on a disc and I could hardly wait to post my pictures on Facebook. People were never going to believe this!

I had already learned this in my bar-going days, but it turns out that it's easy to be a single girl in this world. I usually ate very little during the day and just bought some fruit at a grocery store or stand to get me through. Then I would splurge on nice restaurants for dinner. I always asked for a table for one, but I rarely ate alone. Someone would inevitably notice me eating by myself and start chatting with me. It was nice because I could keep to myself and be left alone when I wanted, but if I made a point of looking around the room and making eye contact, I was almost guaranteed to have someone to chat with.

I have zero sense of direction, so I took a full day just trying to figure out New York's subway system. I stopped at places like Ground Zero, Central Park, and Soho. I took a double-decker bus tour that bored me to tears, but I saw some nice areas. I went to three different Broadway shows. I went to a comedy club one night. I went to the American Girl store (yes, American Girl) and spent over eighty dollars on lip gloss. Before you say it, I'm fully aware that this is a children's store, but it turns out they sell fantastic lip gloss that comes in the most amazing flavours! Hot chocolate was my favourite, but chocolate mint ran a close second. You may think it ridiculous that I spent so much money on lip gloss, but this turned out to be a brilliant move on my part; I am highly addicted to it, and a short time after my trip to New York, they discontinued it. I figure I have enough to last me into my sixties, and hopefully I'll be over my addiction by then. If not, I have more than a few years to figure out what to do.

The most amazing thing that happened to me in New York is that I said goodbye to Clarence. I didn't realize I was doing this, and I don't know how long it would have taken me to realize it, but because I was on this trip alone and forced to make every little decision myself, I was making more decisions in one day than I normally did in a week. It was only then that I realized I had been consulting Clarence about every decision. I would try to decide where to eat dinner and think, "Where would Clarence lead us if he were here?" I would wake up and think, "What would Clarence want to do if he were here?" It was only when I was having these thoughts constantly throughout the day that I realized I was doing it at all. I was making Clarence my God. I was following the direction I thought he would lead as opposed to asking God where He wanted me to go.

I jogged around Central Park, and while I did, I sent Clarence my love, letting him know that I was fully giving him to God. He was no longer mine to lead or follow. I was truly excited for Him to be in the presence of God. I am a selfish person by nature, but not so selfish that I would ever wish him back. Instead, I wished him well in Heaven and let him know that I had let him go. I had to return my focus to Jesus and let Him take His rightful place as my leader.

The rest of my time in New York was spent doing fun things and chatting with God. I never once felt lonely or alone. I returned home just four short days later a new person. I had decided to let go of Clarence—and I was letting go of Greg Dawson, too.

I was done putting all my hopes and energy into any one guy and I was excited to place it in God's hands. I returned to Canada with a newfound energy and excitement for life. I also returned with one very exciting realization: *I am dangerous!* Here I was, just thirty-two years old, young, healthy, and on fire for God. I didn't care about any of my possessions. Status meant nothing to me. Not even losing my job could bring me down. I was on fire for God and ready and willing to go anywhere He asked, do anything He commanded. I had become a very real threat to Satan. I became dangerous to him.

I returned to work and was called into Jo-Ella's office. I was relaxed and ready to hear that my contract had ended. What she did instead was place a piece of paper in front of me, asking me to sign it. It was a full-time contract. I asked about the other two and she said that she had made a business case to hire all three of us.

In less than a year, I had done something that seems nearly impossible in the wonderful world of information technology: I had landed a full-time, permanent position at an outstanding company. Great pay, full benefits, and vacation time—all of this was offered to me, and by someone who had seen me slowly slide into a pit of despair and at times not care if I ever made it out. Jo-Ella had seen my work disintegrate and hadn't given up on me, not even once. I was determined to be a great employee for her. To this day, I don't know if she even realizes how much she did for me, but I spent each hour of my workday trying to do great work for her in return. I had been given a new start.

I did something when I got home that I had never done before. I had my friend Jenn over for dinner. We had never had dinner together before, and we never have since. I had told her a bit about my trip and my photo shoot. She said she wanted to see the pictures, so I invited her to come over for dinner. We hadn't chatted for many months and I had so much to tell her! I hadn't really told anyone else about this, but I finally confessed that I had met a guy whom I had started to fall for and that we were emailing each other regularly. I told her his name and that, as cute and funny as he was, I was giving up on him. She asked me why and I told her that after a month of constant back and forth, he still hadn't even come close to asking me out. He hadn't made a move and I was tired of waiting. Not only that, but I was excited about this decision because I realized how cool it was to be with God and God alone. It sort of felt like "me and God against the world" and I was excited to see where He would lead me.

Jenn got a funny look on her face. "Well, now I'm torn. I feel as though I should tell you something about Greg, but if you're truly in a great place, I don't want to do anything that may ruin that."

I was too excited for anything to bring me down and told her to go for it, that I would be fine.

"Well, here's the thing. It turns out that Greg's mom and my mother-in-law are in the same small group. They get together once a week, and in the past few weeks Greg's mom has mentioned this girl Greg seems to be very interested in. She has asked the group to pray about it, and this girl's name is Jen Lenting."

I did something that I rarely do; I stopped eating. Greg really was interested in me? This wasn't just an email friendship to him? Well, now, what to do with this knowledge? I decided to take the burden off him. I would put myself out there—but only once. If he was interested, he could respond accordingly, and if not, then in my mind I had already let him go, so I wouldn't be devastated by it.

That Monday, I went to work and sent Greg what would potentially be my last email to him. I told him that *Transformers* was playing and I had heard it was a pretty good movie. I finished with, "Are you going to take me or what?"

Greg replied, "*Transformers...* or *The Simpsons*?" I didn't care which movie we saw, I just wanted a chance to talk to him again, to see if the person I was falling head over heels with via email was the same person when I spent face to face time with him.

Greg was going to come over to my place for dinner and then we would head off to the theatre. What actually happened was this: Greg came over for dinner and we began to talk. I confessed that I had heard he was getting baptised at Easter and I was intrigued by that. I asked if he would share with me what had brought him to the place where he wanted to be baptised. He shared his faith with me, and how it came to be. He talked about how God had caught his attention one night. He thought he might be crazy or imagining things, but then God did it again the next day while at work and he knew it had to be God. He told me about how his faith had grown from there and how he was now experiencing a very cool walk with God.

I told Greg that I had sort of a crazy relationship with God myself. He looked at me nervously and asked, "Crazy good?"

"Crazy amazing," I replied.

He seemed both happy and relieved to hear that.

We moved to the backyard and sat on the deck. We spent that entire evening sharing some of the more intense things we had experienced as a result of following God. I was so excited to talk with a guy who "got it." I felt as though I could tell Greg any of my God stories and he wouldn't think I was making it up or losing my mind. He was easy to talk to and very encouraging. We talked until it was dark outside, then Greg thanked me for dinner and the chat and headed home.

I had told my friend Julie that I was having a first date and she was excited for me. She wrote to me on Facebook to ask how it went.

"I don't think he liked me," I said. "We had dinner and ended up talking all night. We didn't end up going to the movie at all, and he didn't try to kiss me when he left."

She promptly told me I was crazy. Apparently the fact that we had missed the movie just to spend hours talking was a great sign. Also, she told me that he sounded like way too much of a gentleman to try kissing me on the first date. Julie decided it was a success.

It turns out she was right. Greg emailed me the next day to say he still owed me a movie and we made plans to get together again. We started to get together once or twice a week and I found our time together intoxicating. I was never as happy as when he was around. Greg hadn't known Clarence, but he had seen him around and knew who he was. He was very mindful of the fact that it was only six months since Clarence had passed away and our dates were very nice—and very hands-off.

It just so happens that God doesn't give us more than we can handle, and I believe He knew I would be a bit of a mess to deal with. Well, He was walking with Greg and preparing Him to be able to handle me. Greg was becoming more than just a boyfriend; he was my friend, my company, and my comfort. This was a lot of pressure for one person to handle and our relationship was tested constantly as time went on. God was about to grow us both individually and as a couple. And growth can be painful.

We hadn't gone on too many dates when we decided to introduce each other to our families. Greg went first. His family had me over for a barbeque one sunny afternoon. I wasn't sure what I was about to walk into, but the moment I arrived I hoped I would never have to leave. His two older sisters were the same age as mine and they were open and inviting. They asked me all sorts of questions and included me in their conversations. We were talking and laughing in no time. His parents seemed loving on sight. I swear I could almost feel them hugging me with their expressions. Even his sisters' husbands were amazing and fun. They were throwing a ball around in the backyard and their children ran around playing, secretly checking me out from around corners. I was taken by how they all seemed to be so close to one another and genuinely enjoyed spending time together. This family looked like a Norman Rockwell painting that had come to life. I wasn't sure how they achieved this, but I wanted in.

A few weeks later, Greg and I went to my parents' home. Everyone sat in the living room when we arrived and were very nice with Greg. We chatted for a while and eventually it started to get dark and we realized we were still talking and nobody had thought to put a light on. I realize this is awful on my part, but at one point in the evening I asked my sister how she and her husband pronounced their last name. For some reason, I always got it mixed up. My dad followed that up with, "How do you spell it again?"

"We've been married for years!" my sister responded, exasperated. "How do you still not know how to say or spell my name?"

One thing my dad and I share is being absentminded. One thing that Greg and my sister share is that they cannot believe just how much.

I was sure that while people weren't actually saying it to me, they were likely commenting on how early it seemed for me to be seeing someone. I felt pressure to show that I was capable of seeing someone new, without that meaning I had somehow forgotten about Clarence. I began to talk about Clarence constantly. I would mention him during conversations, even to the point of throwing random "Clarence memories" into conversations where they didn't fit. I remember mentioning his name so many times once while at Greg's parents' house that even I felt awkward about it. The thing is, the stronger I felt about Greg, the more I felt I had to mention Clarence to even things out. While I thought this would make it easier for Greg, in that people would be more accepting of our relationship, this was not the case.

Greg began to distance himself from me more and more. He made lots of plans with his friends, which left little time for me. He stayed out late into the night with his guy friends, but if he came over to my place to hang out he was yawning by 8:00 p.m., saying he shouldn't stay too much longer. This became very frustrating and I started to wonder if he was the kind of person I wanted to be with. I began to feel foolish for falling for him and it seemed as though our days as a couple were numbered. The tension between us mounted.

Finally Greg asked one evening if he could take me out to dinner. I said sure and that I didn't care where we went, since all the restaurants in Sarnia seemed the same anyway. He replied with, "Great, Harvey's it is!"

I knew he was trying to be funny with the fast food quip, but even his humour had lost its effect on me. I didn't bite and replied, "Fine with me."

When our date night came, he picked me up and took me across the border to the Olive Garden. I really liked the Olive Garden, and even more so because I hardly ever went there.

Conversation was short between us and you could cut the tension with a knife. I began to realize he was going to break up with me and I dreaded the thought of the car ride home and having to wait to cross at the border. I was also bitter as I realized I would now have a bad memory tied to this restaurant. I felt a little heartsick because as much as he had annoyed me lately, I still cared for him deeply. The thought of not having him around made me feel ill.

We ordered and waited uncomfortably for our food. I kept waiting for him to just come out and say it, but he didn't. Our food came and Greg dove right into his meal. I took a bite or two but couldn't taste a thing. I asked him if we could talk about what was going on.

"Not now," Greg said. "Let's not ruin our meal."

I knew what that meant. Why didn't he just say the words and get it over with? Not hearing them seemed worse somehow. I just sat staring at my plate. I could feel a big fat tear roll down my face.

Greg realized I was crying and I said, "Please, can we just do this? There's nothing you can say that will be worse than what I'm imagining."

Again, he refused and continued to eat. Finally I couldn't stand it any longer.

"Listen, I know you're planning to end things with me tonight, and that's okay," I told him. "I just want to get this off my chest before you do; I think I've fallen in love with you. I know that doesn't change anything, I just wanted to say that—"

"Jen, I love you."

I looked at him with an almost angry expression. "What?"

How on earth was he saying this to me?

He put his fork down. "I love you. It's been so hard because you talk about Clarence all the time. I understand he was your husband and of course you love him and I don't blame you for that at all, but every time his name comes up it makes me feel like nothing. I guess I'm being selfish, but I just don't know if—"

I cut him off at that point and asked him to stop. He tried to explain further that he felt like a bad person for saying that and again I told him to just please stop talking. I broke into tears, explaining that I was only mentioning Clarence's name as a way of protecting him. I told him how ridiculous I had felt mentioning Clarence so many times when we'd been at his parents' house. I didn't know what else to do, and the more I fell for Greg, the more I did it.

"Jen, I didn't know Clarence personally, but I knew of him and everyone who knew him speaks so highly of him. Everyone loves him, and of course you love him. I don't think anyone would ever think differently. You had a great marriage and people knew it. Saying his name more doesn't mean you loved him more."

I knew that Greg was right and hearing those words felt so freeing. I apologized for ever making him feel that way, and he apologized for distancing himself; he just hadn't known how else to deal with it.

We left the restaurant and Greg suggested we go for a drive. We drove around for a while and let it sink in that we were each in love with the other. I admitted that I was so grateful he hadn't ruined that restaurant for me, and then we laughed at how I had sat there having a mental breakdown while Greg still managed to happily eat his spaghetti and meatballs.

As we were about to cross the border, I said, "You know, had you broken up with me, I was going to tell the border guard you were carrying drugs."

"Yep," Greg replied. "And you were carrying them for me in secret places."

I laughed out loud and realized that we were back. Greg dropped me off at home and kissed me tenderly before heading off. Things were about to change for us.

The Game Is the Same, But the Rules Have Changed

Our makeout sessions started to become intense, but we didn't have sex. While I hadn't waited for marriage the first time around, I also hadn't had a relationship with God the way I did now. I wanted to honour that relationship. My dilemma was this: what thirty-one-year-old guy was going to wait for marriage? I was well aware that this could end our relationship and I dreaded having this talk with Greg, but as hard as I had fallen for him, I still loved God more. I really felt as though this was something I had to do.

One day when Greg was over at my place, he sat on the kitchen counter and I stood nearby. I told him that I had to run something by him and he wouldn't like it.

"Uh-oh, should I get my keys?"

"Yes," I replied seriously. "You may want to leave when you hear this."

I handed him the key.

He stopped joking around. "What's going on?"

"Well, here's the thing. I know we've been going a little further lately and I haven't given you any indication that I wouldn't have sex with you. While I didn't wait in the past, I also didn't know God the way I do now. I want to honour my relationship with him and I don't intend to have sex before I'm married again."

I waited for Greg to jump off the counter and bolt for the door, but he didn't do that. What he did do was reach over, pick up the phone, and fake dial it.

"Hi, Mom?" he said into the receiver. "Yeah, you're *really* going to like this one."

He smiled at me and then said that he completely understood. His own relationship with God had him feeling that way, too. He would respect that and we both agreed to try not to tempt each other beyond the point of no return. In a society where everyone is told you need to "test the goods before you buy" and that "bad sex will ruin a marriage so you need to make sure the other person is good at it before you marry them," I found a man who was the proverbial needle in a haystack. He was willing to date me without having sex and decide through that alone whether or not I was the one for him.

When it comes to women, our culture seems to place more emphasis on purity. We tell young girls to save themselves for marriage and that their husband will appreciate that about them. I think it very much goes both ways. That one act on Greg's part made me respect him more than any man I've ever known. What mattered was not how compatible we were physically, but that he was willing to stand up and be an honourable, God-loving, God-fearing man when it came to his relationship with me. That told me that if he were to be my husband one day, he would be a husband I could love and respect, and his opinion would be one I could trust and value. We began to see the strength in each other's faith and our relationship became stronger still.

This didn't mean we were guaranteed easy times. Not by a longshot!

I seemed to cry a lot in the months to come and it was always when Greg was with me. It started to occur to me that nobody had the ability to make me cry like he did. Why was I always so miserable with him? Why did he have this effect on me? I began to think that he was becoming quite the jerk. Greg wasn't moved at all by my tears. He said that he quickly became immune to them and that he just ignored me when I cried. I found this frustrating.

A couple of months went by and it became almost unbearable to be around him. Again, I wondered why we were together. I often prayed to God about Greg. I had been convinced we had been prayerfully brought together and I couldn't imagine why God would bring me together with someone who would make me so miserable. I started to think about breaking up with him.

One day while in prayer, it suddenly came to me why I was

crying all the time. I was so relieved at the revelation that I could hardly wait to share it with Greg.

We went out for dinner one night and I said, "I have to explain something to you."

He braced himself for yet another lengthy story of mine, because that's how I roll... I talk in stories. I explained how one day I had been feeling incredibly alone and sad. I began to cry, but then realized how silly it was, since there was nobody around to care or comfort me. I stopped crying immediately and didn't cry again. With the exception of the odd tear, I basically bottled up all my emotion. When Greg came along, I suddenly had someone to voice my concerns to. I could share my aches and pains with him and, more importantly, I could cry and not be alone while I did it. All of this pent-up emotion came out... but only when Greg was around. I mistook that as meaning that Greg made me cry, when in reality Greg's presence gave me the freedom to cry!

Greg had a funny look on his face.

"Did you know this?" I asked.

"I thought it might be something like that, but I didn't know for sure, and I didn't think you would want to hear it from me if that was the case."

I apologized for unleashing all this on him, and then for blaming him as though it was his fault! He said it was okay. He was glad that I at least knew where it was coming from now.

Seriously, I don't know how Greg stayed with me. No person should have to carry so much of another person's burdens, and yet he chose to stick it out. Greg would always say to me, "It's okay, I know that you're crazy," and I would laugh and reply, "You love my crazy." The thing was, I never actually knew at the time that I was truly and completely crazy. I can see now that in the months following Clarence's death, while I felt as though I was getting through things as well as could be expected, I had still managed to jump on the crazy train—and the ride wasn't over yet.

I still cried, but at least I was beginning to understand my tears. Tears of loss or heartache would sometimes randomly resurface, but I'd shed tears of complete amazement and awe. I was having a hard time comprehending all the things God was doing in my life. Whenever I really thought about it all, I was brought to tears. I really cannot comprehend why anyone would be hesitant to accept a God who's so loving, so patient, so forgiving, and so ridiculously crazy in the way He works.

You Show Me a Prayer and I'll Show You the Power in It

While Clarence was in palliative care, I sometimes left his room just to wander around and stretch my legs. I also had to take Sixx outside every so often. On one such occasion, I met a girl who was about the same age as me in the hallway. Her mother was dying of cancer as well. She asked if I'd mind bringing Sixx into her room for a visit since her mother missed her own dog so much. She thought seeing a dog might cheer her up. I brought Sixx in and her mother petted him and smiled.

What I didn't know was that this girl, who I met under such sad circumstances and barely knew, ended up calling her good friend to ask a favour.

"I want you and your family to stop praying for my mom," she said.

"What? Why?"

"My mom is at peace with this. She knows she's going to die and she's older. She doesn't want to be in this state anymore. Instead, I want you to pray for this young couple next door. They're only thirty-one years old and he has cancer. They seem like a great couple."

Around this time, there was a small group getting together weekly. One of the ladies, Mikki, asked her friends if they would please pray for her son's friend, Clarence. She, along with the other women in her group, none of whom knew Clarence or me, also started praying for us.

Clarence passed away and Mikki asked her small group if they would please continue to pray for his young widow, and they did so. She shared that I was in my early thirties and loved the Lord, then asked that they continue to lift me up in their prayers to Him.

One day while I was out walking Sixx, I wiped out badly on some ice hidden beneath the snow. My knee (which I'd had ACL/MCL surgery on less than six months earlier) bent this way, then that, as I went down. I was certain that I had ruined it and would need surgery again. While I lay on the ground crying, not knowing how I was going to get home, trying to hold onto the leash with my anxious Doberman prancing around at the end of it, a young boy walked right by me and didn't even stop to ask if I was okay.

I began to wonder if I would have to crawl home on my hands and one good leg when a jogger came running up to me and asked what had happened. I explained that I thought I had blown out my knee and didn't think I could get up. He told me to wait and he ran home to get his car. He picked me and my dog up and drove me home. He left without asking for a thing in return.

My neighbour, who could be an amazing detective because she sees and hears everything, noticed him dropping me off. I explained to her what had happened and said I wished I knew who he was because I would love to send him a thank-you note. I should have known she would know who he was. She told me his name and the street he lived on. She mentioned that he and his wife were our age and had a young baby. I sent them a thank-you note with a Wal-Mart gift card.

Before I met Greg, he had been living alone and working in Toronto, but his parents convinced him that, while he may be having fun, he wasn't getting ahead at all. Why didn't he consider returning home and going back to school? They said he could live at their house to save money, enabling him to buy a nice place once he graduated and got a better paying job. Greg wisely accepted his parents' counsel and enrolled in a three-year Human Resources program at Lambton College. He worked part-time in NOVA's accounting department during his work terms.

One night, Greg went for a walk, as he often did to get some alone time. His mom, Neta, recalls sitting on the couch and seeing him walk past the front window. His shoulders were a little slumped and she worried about how he was doing. She was in Mikki's small group and had been praying for this young widow who lived in the same small town and knew that she was in her early thirties, loved

God wholeheartedly, and, she assumed, would be feeling all alone in the world. Neta began to pray for her son and asked God if it would be possible for this boy of hers to meet this girl she had been praying for. Maybe we could each remove the loneliness for the other and maybe even be good for each other?

The night that Greg and I met at Jeremy and Teresa's place, they had actually intended to set him up with someone else. They weren't so great at playing matchmakers; they told Greg they wanted to set him up with this girl, but they didn't tell her the plan. She spent her time hanging out with her friends and she and Greg barely got a chance to talk.

When Greg returned to his parents' place that night, his dad asked how it had gone. Greg said they hadn't really gotten a chance to meet, but he had met someone else unexpectedly. His dad had been reading the paper at the time and slowly pulled it down.

"Maybe God has another plan for you," his father said, then quickly put the paper back in front of his face.

Greg and I started to email at work and a little over a month later we went on our first date. When this happened, his parents were actually away on an Alaskan vacation. Neta called home to see how everyone was doing and to say they were having a good time. Greg's sister Deanna told his mom that he had gone on several dates in a row. Her husband had set him up on one, a friend on another, and someone else set him up on a third date, all in a span of a week or two.

After our date, Greg apparently went home and said, "I think I may have found the one." His friends tried to convince him to keep his options open in case he was wrong about me, but he talked to his brother-in-law, Mark, and Mark said he should do the right thing and let the other girls know. Greg then called them and told them he'd had a good time, but he had met someone else and he wouldn't be able to see them again. His mom was so excited to hear this news that she started asking questions. Deanna said she didn't know much, but she thought I had lost my husband fairly recently to cancer. Greg's mom knew right away that it was me; God was answering prayers that had been spoken for both Greg and me. She was excited to meet me.

I didn't know that Greg's parents knew anything about me the first time I met them, but they had known my story for quite some time and actually felt a bit attached to this young wife, then widow, and now girlfriend to their son. They had been more involved in my life than I could have ever imagined.

After dating for a short while, Greg's oldest sister, Davina, called me to say that she had something to share with me. She had been talking on the phone with her girlfriend, the one whose mother had been in palliative care at the same time as Clarence, and mentioned that her brother Greg was seeing someone now. Her friend, who was very fond of Greg, was excited to hear the news. She asked about me and, in the course of their conversation, they started to put things together.

"I have a few questions for you and I want you to answer with yes or no, okay?" Davina then asked her friend if the girl in the hospital with the dog had been named Jennifer. Her friend thought so, but wasn't certain. She asked if the dog had been a Doberman.

"Yes."

Had her husband been a paramedic?

"Yes, I'm pretty sure he was."

"Well, that's the girl who's dating my brother!" Davina said.

That's not the craziest part of the story. Her mom had been expected to die while she was in palliative care. She randomly and inexplicably got better and returned home. She lived another year before finally passing.

I attended another family event at the Dawsons', but this time Deanna's in-laws were there as well. They were a great family and easy to talk to. It was during this initial meeting that Deanna's brother-in-law realized that he recognized me. He asked if I had a Doberman and we discovered that he had been the jogger who helped me up and drove me home. This was just one more connection that had been made within this family, many months before I even knew any of them.

You'll never be able to convince me that there isn't power in prayer. I believe with my whole heart that Greg and I didn't randomly bump into each other. We were very clearly brought together.

Greg had told me that the day God grabbed his attention for the second time, there was urgency in it. He decided quickly to confess his sins, profess his faith, and get baptised. I often wonder if that urgency had to do with the plan God was working out for us. Had he not acted quickly and decided to get baptised, Jeremy never would have told me about his baptism and I never would have thought twice about him. I'd already had a strong crush on another guy when I met him and had I not known about Greg's recent faithful step, there would have been nothing important differentiating him from this other person—initially, at least. Had God been prompting Greg to hurry up and move in his faith so that he'd be ready for me and I'd be more attracted to him? I suppose I'll never know, but somehow I think that even the timing of Greg's baptism was spirit-led.

Two Becoming One

Even though God has His hand in the mix and can make all things possible, we're still very much capable of messing those things up. Greg and I had our hundredth (it seemed) disagreement one day while driving to Strathroy together to visit my family. We found this hour-long drive difficult because, for some reason, my brain had decided that when I had him trapped in a car for any length of time, that was a good opportunity to bring up any issues.

This day was no different and Greg was being very quiet and unresponsive. It was annoying and I asked him what his deal was.

"I can't be *on* for you all the time, Jen," he replied.

I wanted to punch him in the face. I pulled over the car and asked what his problem was. He said nothing and that he was just tired. I realized he wasn't going to tell me, so I started to drive again.

"I'm not sure why you're acting so sketchy," I said. "It's not as though I'm asking for a proposal or anything. I just want to know that you're in this relationship as much as I am."

"Whoa, whoa, whoa! I'm not ready to get married yet."

"Fine, because I wasn't asking. But one day, I would like to be proposed to."

"Well," he said, "maybe *I* want to be proposed to."

I snapped back. "Fine, will you marry me?"

"No, I'm not ready."

"Good. Consider yourself asked. It won't happen again."

That was the end of the discussion and November 5 would forever go down in history as the day I proposed to Greg. I don't even remember what started that argument, but as always, we were laughing on our way home.

We spent our first Christmas together with both Greg's parents and then mine. While with his family, Greg handed me a gift. I opened it and saw a brown leatherbound book with the following scripture written on the front: *"'For I know the plans I have for you,' declares the Lord, 'plans to prosper you and not to harm you, plans to give you hope and a future'"* (Jeremiah 29:11).

I burst into tears. I couldn't stop crying and had to go to the bathroom to pull myself together. I'm sure his whole family thought I was completely insane, but what I was unable to express through all my tears was that in reading those words, I'd felt as though God was whispering them to me. I knew they were true. I had seen how my despair and complete brokenness had turned into joy for the Lord. In walking me through the past year, with all its highs and lows, I had developed a deeper understanding of God and there was a joy and peace that came with that. These very truthful words being presented to me, and by Greg no less, caused such complete relief and joy to wash over me that I didn't know what to do. All I could do was cry.

The end of 2007 rolled around and Greg and I spent New Year's Eve, which also happened to be his birthday, in Toronto with his friends. I was nervous to meet them because they were such a tight group and I knew their opinions of me would go a long way. Not to mention, I really wanted to like the people he cared about the most. In hindsight, I'm not sure why I was worried. Greg was such a great guy, it only stood to reason that all his friends would be great as well. They were incredibly friendly and inviting and we had an amazing time together.

Greg and I took our first trip together and went to Chicago for my birthday weekend in March. He got a speeding ticket as we were literally two minutes from the airport. We were looking at the signs so closely that we hadn't noticed that the speed limit had dropped. I was worried that this would put him in a funk and the whole weekend would be affected, but I was pleasantly surprised by his very calm reaction. He just thanked God that we had the means to pay. We had a cold, fun weekend and learned that we could travel together quite easily. It turned out that I could be in a car with him, or a plane, or exploring a new place... and no matter where we were or what we were doing, his company was always the highlight for me.

The summer of 2008 had us taking a trip to British Columbia to attend his good friends Pete and Alex's wedding. Again, it reinforced for me that he had great friends. Though he was in the wedding party and much of the trip was spent hanging out with the boys and doing "pre-wedding stuff," Greg was thoughtful and made sure to spend time here and there with me. I found a gym nearby and spent time each day working out; his sister Davina, her husband Mike, and myself had all decided to do a triathlon that summer.

Greg and I seemed to do a good job of striking a balance between seeing each other and giving each other enough space to do our own thing. Again, it was nice to see that we travelled well together. It was a beautiful wedding and we made it there and back intact as a couple.

A month later, we were off to take part in the triathlon. We were to head straight from there to a resort up north with Greg's entire family. Again, this was a big deal. This would be an entire week of hanging out with parents and sisters, spouses and children. Greg had almost taken a girlfriend to this resort with his family once before, but ended up uninviting her last-minute as he realized she wasn't the one and he didn't want to spend that week with his family and her. I think he was just as nervous about this week as I was, wondering if he would get jitters and have to cancel on me. He didn't and we had an amazing time.

Both Mike and Davina ran a fantastic race and had very respectable times. While I was a strong swimmer, I hadn't swam in months. I also didn't ride a bicycle. I'd gone for one twenty-five-kilometre ride a few weeks before the race and decided that would be good enough. I had never done a swim, bike ride, then run back-to-back-to-back. I knew I could do each one individually, but all together? I wasn't sure how that would go. I completed the swim near the end of my pack, but not last, which was encouraging. I began the bike ride and couldn't believe how many massive hills there were! I had no clue how to work my gears, or even which gears I should use while climbing hills, so I just stuck to the same gear the whole time. I later learned that this was the equivalent of riding a kid's bike up a big hill... very ineffective. No kidding!

I was disappointed that one of the rules was you couldn't wear headphones and listen to music. It turns out I didn't need to worry about that. I was the very last person biking, so some teenage boy drove behind me in a car with music blaring and picked up the pylons as I passed them. I like to think that was God showing me love with a little music along the way.

I finished the bike ride and decided that I didn't like the shorts I was wearing, so I took them off and put on some capris. I had a girl nearby take my picture so I could prove I had at least made it this far. Someone asked me what my time was and I said, "Oh, I'm not done, I have to do the run still." They looked at me as though I was crazy. Everyone around me was finished and eating sandwiches. I took a drink of water and then was off and running. Again, as I passed the water tables, they began to fold them up and put them away. Clearly, I was the very last person to complete this triathlon. I didn't care. I had said I would do it without stopping and I wasn't going to stop.

They were going to take the "Finish" sign down, but Davina asked the lady to please keep it up a little longer because she knew for a fact that there was still someone out on the course. Greg began to get worried, so he started walking the course to see if he could find me. He met up with me at the six-kilometre mark; I had just one kilometre to go. He had this big grin on his face when he saw me.

"I can't stop now," I explained.

"Don't stop," he said. "You can do this. I'll run with you."

He didn't have running shoes on, but he ran alongside me anyway. A few minutes in, he said, "Wow, I'm out of shape, you finish this and I'll meet you at the end."

I ran in to sympathetic cheers. The entire Dawson family cheered loudly at the finish line. I was so red in the face that I looked as though I would explode. Everything in me hurt, but the sense of accomplishment was awesome and we all laughed at how ridiculous I was to take part in a race like this so incredibly unprepared. I'm stubborn, though, and when I get something in my head, I'll do it whether I'm ready or not. That has been both a gift and a curse for me, but that's who I am. It's part of what makes me crazy and part of what makes my life so fun and unpredictable—and admittedly, sometimes dangerous.

I learned that day that if you aren't going to come in first, you may as well come in last. At least it makes for a funny story to share later. Whoever heard about or remembered the person who came in thirty-fifth out of fifty? Exactly.

We made our way to the resort and I felt ill. I slept the entire first afternoon away, but was fine by dinnertime.

One very cool thing happened while we were there. After Clarence passed away, I wore his wedding band on my finger, and then held it in place with my wedding band. I liked having our wedding bands together like that, and I even liked the look of it. Once Greg and I started to get serious, I didn't stop wearing those bands; I just moved them over to my other hand to signify that I wasn't married. I didn't really intend to ever stop wearing those bands, to be honest. One afternoon, as Greg and I played on the basketball court, the bands kept slipping off my hand. I hadn't lost weight and it wasn't the heat, because I had been this hot while playing sports before and they had never seemed loose. On this day, though, I couldn't keep them on my finger for more than a few seconds at a time.

Greg finally asked, "What's wrong with your rings?"

"I think I'm being told it's time to take them off."

I put them in my pocket, and later in a drawer, and I never placed them on my finger again. I think it was during this week that I became fully available to Greg in both of our minds. Something changed for us that day.

There was a little display setup at the resort with jewellery and various knickknacks. The one thing that jumped out at me was this cute little sock puppet monkey. I don't know why, but I found it so cute that I couldn't stop going back to it. I didn't buy it, though. I thought that would seem childish and silly. Well, Greg snuck back and bought that sock monkey for me. He surprised me with it later that night. I love that toy. It acts as a constant reminder to me that Greg is very perceptive, paying attention to my wants and needs—even the smallest, silliest ones—and that he doesn't think twice about doing things he knows will bring me happiness. That sock monkey sits in my bedroom. Every time I see him there, I'm reminded of how amazing God has been to me in my life, and how loved I am.

Wedding Bells or Living Hell?

The summer passed and I was confused. I was now thirty-three years old and I had been very clear when Greg and I first started dating that I wasn't bitter toward men and I hadn't been burned in any way. I'd had a great marriage and it had ended, but that didn't leave me fearing marriage. I knew how incredible married life could be and I was convinced God would have me marry again one day. I didn't think that just because Greg was the first person I dated that he would necessarily be the one, so I didn't want him to feel pressured. I did want him to know that my intention was to marry again one day and if at any point he realized I wasn't the one he wanted to marry, he was to please tell me right away. I was at an age where game playing was neither fun nor acceptable. I wanted him to be real and honest about who he was so I could determine if he would be good for me, and I intended to do the same for him. Greg said that he, too, wanted to be married one day and he didn't date just for the sake of dating; he was looking for his future wife.

We had been together for just over a year, which in my mind was plenty of time at our age to know whether or not we could spend the rest of our lives together. He seemed to be making no move to propose and I started to feel as though he was stringing me along. It wasn't long before bitterness crept in. The days turned into weeks and the more bitter I became, the more Greg started to bother me. Again, I cried out to God, asking why He would bring someone into my life and allow things to get so good, just to have them come to a grinding halt.

We were nearing the fall of 2008 and all I could think was, *If he doesn't propose by the end of the year, I'll end things.* I didn't want to spend another year with someone who wasn't going to be my husband. My only challenge was figuring out when to break up with someone whose birthday was on December 31. Breaking up during the Christmas season seems tacky, but doing it in the New Year would be so close to his birthday. I wasn't sure what to do. I had been excited about this relationship, too. I had been certain for so many reasons and for so long that Greg was the one. I had been picturing our wedding day and I had images of a church full of people worshiping God and loving Him the way Greg and I did, then saying our vows before God and these people.

I remember feeling so low one day after church that I took my Bible and went down to the water. I decided that I wouldn't leave until God told me very clearly what I was supposed to do. I read from the Bible almost frantically, certain that a word or a verse would jump out at me and give me some sense of direction.

I happened to be on-call that week and my pager went off. I didn't care. I ignored it and continued to read. I wasn't leaving this place for anyone or anything until God helped me figure things out. About fifteen minutes later, the pager went off again. It was getting dark outside and I could barely see the words on the page. Frustrated, and feeling guilty about leaving this page unanswered, I closed my Bible and headed to the car. I turned the radio on and was surprised to hear a new song on 88.3. I listened to the lyrics and nearly drove off the road. It was a song called "One Step at a Time" by Jordin Sparks. The song spoke of how there's no need to rush love, that it will unfold as it should, and to just take one step at a time.

Somehow this made complete sense to me. It was going to happen when it was supposed to happen—and no sooner. There was my answer. Again I remembered, "Patience. Faith. Love." I was being reminded of the "patience" part.

I got home and checked my page. There were two, actually. The first was from a coworker in need of computer assistance and then a second one stating that I could ignore the first; they had gotten an answer to their question. There was no doubt in my mind that God knew I wasn't going anywhere until He answered me, but sometimes the answers come in different forms. I have had thoughts in my head that I knew I would never come up with on my own. I have heard lyrics in songs, interviews on the radio, read verses in the Bible, and even had visions. God doesn't leave prayers unanswered. We are told to pray without ceasing (1 Thessalonians 5:17) and it is my experience that God answers all prayers. The answer may be yes, no, or later... but it will be answered, just the same.

You would think this would have been enough and I'd have let the whole marriage thing go, but a few short weeks later I fretted over it again. I just didn't understand why Greg seemed to be taking his sweet time. Did he not see how good we were together? Did he not want children? Was he forgetting that I was nearly two years older than him and that I didn't have all the time in the world?

While driving one day, I heard a voice as clear as if there was a person sitting next to me in the car. It said, *"You said you wanted this wedding to be about me. I'm not ready yet."* I made my way home with shaking hands and sat in the driveway for a while. God was working out a plan! I had prayed about having a God-honouring wedding and He intended to move in someone's heart to prepare them for that day, I was sure of it.

It was on this day that I stopped worrying about getting a proposal from Greg. In fact, I really didn't think about it at all. I knew that God was at work and we needed to abide by His timing, not our own.

I became happy just dating Greg again and felt more lighthearted than I had in many months. We began to have more fun together and I was grateful to be able to just enjoy myself instead of worrying about what the future looked like and wasting all the good moments in our present together.

Greg went away for a weekend in November to attend a "Promise Keepers" event. I was excited for him to go. The night before he was to leave, we ate out at a restaurant. While we were eating, he slipped me a card. It basically said that he loved me and would be thinking of me while he was away. That was such a small gesture, but I don't think men comprehend just how much it means for a woman to be told these things. He could have just said the words and I would have appreciated it just the same, but the fact that he took the time to get a card and write it down meant he had put that much more thought into it.

As per usual, I began to cry. It seems that a few months of not crying meant that I would spend the rest of my life making up for lost time! I managed to pull myself together and we had a nice dinner. He seemed extra attentive that night for some reason. I couldn't put my finger on it, but he was different. He took me home afterward and we said our goodbyes.

It turned out they had a fantastic weekend and his brother-in-law Mike ended up having an incredible experience where he felt the presence of God and understood suddenly what it was all about. He came home incredibly excited to share the news with his wife and the rest of the family. He had just caught fire for God!

Greg and I chatted on Monday via email and then made plans to get together for dinner at my place so I could hear all about his weekend. We had a nice dinner, and afterward he said he needed to check his email for a minute. He went to the office and I randomly decided to brush and floss my teeth. I really have no idea why, because I didn't normally do that right after dinner.

Greg came to find me in the bathroom and seemed flustered that I was taking so long. He told me to hurry up and join him in the living room. I went to the living room and turned the TV on, then sat on the couch and faced him. He sat up and started telling me more about the weekend and what they had heard while they were there. I was trying to listen, but if there's one thing I'm bad at, it's paying attention to someone while the TV is on. I sensed that he really wanted to share something with me, so I turned the TV off and apologized. I asked if he would start again.

He began to explain the messages they had heard and how the speakers talked a lot about men and women and their roles within relationships. He said that as they spoke, it was confirmed to him that we had a really great relationship and he was glad we had found each other. Before we started dating, he had been getting frustrated because he was thirty and most of his friends were either dating or married and he hadn't found anyone who mattered to him in that way. While reading the Bible with his brother-in-law one night, a passage jumped out at him: *"Until now you have not asked for anything in my name. Ask and you will receive, and your joy will be complete"* (John 16:24). He explained that while he wanted to meet someone and one day marry, he had never really taken that to God and asked for this to happen in his life. So, he went for a walk one night, feeling very low about still being alone. Then he remembered this verse and he prayed in Jesus' name that he would meet a great girl who loved God the way he did, who he could love and marry. Shortly after that prayerful walk, he ran into me. He believed that God had answered his prayer with me.

Then he got down on one knee and asked if I would spend the rest of my life with him.

I looked at him in shock. "Are you kidding me?"

He didn't move.

I said again, this time sounding almost angry. "Are you kidding me?"

He looked a little confused and shook his head. I felt as though I was hovering over us and could see everything from above. I heard my tone of voice and I was trying to yell at myself, "Shut up, fool!" But the words wouldn't come out.

I said for the third and final time, "Are you kidding me?"

Then I cried and held my finger out. I don't really know why the angry "are you kidding me" kept coming out, but we laugh about it now. Greg said he was glad that he had confided in a couple of his friends that he was planning to propose to me. They had warned him that my reaction could be any number of things since I would likely be in shock, and not to get offended if my reaction wasn't what he expected. I was grateful he had such great friends who gave such wise advice!

We hugged and kissed and hugged some more. I think five or more minutes passed before I finally said, "Wait... did I say yes?"

Greg smiled. "I took that as a yes."

It was then that I officially told him that it would be my honour to become Mrs. Greg Dawson.

In a moment of panic, I asked if he had prayed about this before asking me. Less than a month before, God had very clearly told me that He wasn't ready for this yet. Greg said that he had been praying about it nonstop and he was sure this was the right time. I had come to know Greg's faith as being steady and true, so I felt at ease that this was, in fact, the right time.

Let the wedding planning begin!

Do You Take This Man?

Greg and I went back to the Olive Garden to plan a few details for our wedding. Would it be inside or out? Which church would we get married in? Who should marry us? When should it happen? And so on. It made sense to go there since this was where we'd nearly parted ways and then realized we were, in fact, in love with each other.

Decisions seemed to come easily, as did most of the planning. Everything just naturally fell into place, which only confirmed that this was the right move for us.

Most brides have dreams of having the best dress, the most beautiful decorations, and the biggest and most memorable party. These concerns weren't my focus. Maybe that's why the decisions were so easy to make; I didn't care if my wedding day looked better than other peoples' weddings.

My focus was on planning the most God-honouring wedding possible. I had visions of everyone singing worship music so loudly that we caused the church's roof to tremble. I could just imagine what a sweet sound that would be to God's ears. Greg quickly put a stop to that idea. I was confused. Wasn't he the one who had said that he'd prayed for a godly wife just before meeting me? Wasn't he the one who was always so steady in his faith? Why could he not see the joy in this? After talking about it for a while, he said that he understood my desire, but that I had to remember that there would be lots of people attending who neither knew nor cared to know God. They wouldn't be worshipping Him, but rather standing around awkwardly, hating every moment of it. I knew he was right and the idea was scrapped. We decided to have a low-key wedding that was fairly standard. God was of course mentioned in our vows and we both wholeheartedly invited Him into our lives as a married couple.

The reception, too, was pretty standard—but fun. We rented a photo booth and people had a blast having their pictures taken. They got to keep a strip of photos for themselves while they pasted the second strip into a book, writing comments beside it that we could keep and look at later.

The one thing that was really unique, I would say, was my speech. I realized when I spoke at Clarence's funeral that if I was completely obedient and willing, God would give me the words to say in front of a large crowd. I was also aware that there are two times in life when people's hearts tend to be a little more tender—at weddings and funerals. You can tell people how you feel about them at weddings, expressing your love, and it's somehow okay. But if you said those same words any other time, it would be awkward and difficult to hear.

I spent many months trying to prepare what to say, all the while telling God that I would give Him the ultimate say. While taking Sixx out to a field and letting him run free, I walked and talked to myself, thinking of something sweet for each person I wanted to address. I thought I had the perfect speech at one point. There were just enough humorous and loving comments to make it appreciated and memorable.

The next time I walked Sixx, I went through it again to make sure I had it memorized. As I said it, entire portions suddenly didn't sound right to me. They almost hurt my ears, if that makes sense. I decided to cut those pieces, but then thought it sounded too short and choppy. I asked God to help me fill those spots, and by the end of the walk I had new material to replace the old. This happened repeatedly until in the end I realized I hadn't written my speech at all. I said it out loud a few times and knew it was good, and right, and true. I just had no idea how it would be received, and whether or not I would have the nerve to speak it when the time came.

I almost didn't have to worry. We were just a few months away from the wedding when Greg had yet another bad experience with Sixx. Sixx initially liked Greg very much, but once Greg started coming around more often, there became a bit of a jealousy issue and Sixx made a point of standing between Greg and me whenever he got the chance. He challenged Greg constantly and was still very much dominant over me. I hired a trainer to come to my home and watch how we interacted. He helped a great deal, but some of these behaviours had been going on since day one and I found it virtually impossible to change them.

In an email one day, Greg told me that he thought I should give Sixx back to the breeder to see if he could find another home for him. This was a bit of a shock to me. I knew Greg didn't particularly like Sixx, and vice versa, but I just figured we would make it work somehow. We met for dinner at my place that night and I told Greg I felt as though Sixx and I were a package deal. Greg was furious, taking that to mean that I cared more about Sixx than him. That wasn't the case; I just never really thought I would have to choose.

We came to a bit of a standstill and knew that until this was resolved, there would be no wedding. It became a match of "If you loved me, you would tolerate the dog" versus "If you loved me, you wouldn't choose an animal over me." We both turned to friends and family for advice and guidance—and maybe that was a mistake. The two sides were very much divided between dog lovers and non-dog lovers. One group was horrified at the thought of being asked to part with a dog, and the other group didn't see what the big deal was; why would you cancel a marriage and a future together over something like this?

We both became frustrated and said and did hurtful things to each other. It was a tough time, to say the least. We decided to spend a few days apart to get our heads straight and really think about all this. The not knowing was killing me. I hated having our relationship up in the air and really just wanted to know how things would end. I asked him over one night after we had both cooled down a bit. We agreed that he wouldn't leave until we made a decision one way or the other. Again, we used the same arguments and found ourselves at a standstill.

Greg left to use the washroom and I looked over at Sixx, who was conveniently lying very quietly, being an angel just to make it more difficult. I cried out from the depths of my soul to God, asking God, "Why is this so difficult for me? For the first three years, I would have gladly given this dog away, but my own pride and stubbornness made me keep him. Now someone is asking me to give him away and suddenly I can't bear the thought. Why, God?"

In that moment, I knew.

"I know why I'm having a hard time parting with Sixx," I said when Greg returned. "He's my backup plan. You have a lot of really close friends and you do your best to make time for all of them. I don't have a social circle like that. I'm not naïve, Greg. I can imagine that we will get married and, while we may live together, not a lot will change. You will be out most nights hanging out with your friends and I'll be home alone, back where I started. I'll be lonely."

Greg sat beside me on the couch. "Jen, look at me. I want to marry you. I want to spend the rest of my life with you. If you're feeling lonely in our marriage, then I'm doing something wrong as a husband. If that happens, I want you to tell me and I'll make changes until you stop feeling lonely. I don't want you to feel as though you have to enter into a marriage with me needing a backup plan. If you need a backup plan, what does that say about our relationship? I don't have a backup plan. You are my only plan. I want to be yours."

I knew Greg was right. The truth was that Clarence and I had kept Sixx out of pride, not wanting to admit that we were in over our heads. Once it was just Sixx and me, I kept him for purely selfish reasons. I didn't have a yard nearly big enough for him to run in. I didn't have the time or energy to walk him even close to as much as he needed. Sixx and I butted heads so much because he had an incredible amount of pent-up energy and I didn't help him to release it.

I called Manuel from Vixenvale Kennels to see if he would take his dog back. Manuel and his family took care of Sixx for me anytime I went on vacation and they loved him as much as I did. He said they would keep him until they found a great home for him.

As it turns out, a lady who owned a female Doberman from Manuel was looking for a playmate for her. Manuel asked this lady if she would like to have Sixx for a weekend to see how he made out at her place. By the end of the weekend, she said she wouldn't give Sixx back even if Manuel wanted her to. She had fallen in love with this energetic dog, and so had her dog. She had a large property and the two dogs ran and played constantly. She sent Manuel a picture of the two dogs sleeping together, literally spooning one another.

I don't regret giving Sixx away, even though I do miss him sometimes. I just regret that I kept him longer than I should have to fill my own selfish needs, when he could have been living the good life sooner. I also gave away my two cats, but that was more their decision than ours. When we tried to move them over to our new home, they lost their minds. They screamed for three days straight, and by the end we decided maybe that was a sign. I managed to find a home that would take them both so they could stay together. This family had several children and they asked if the cats would like sleeping in bed with the kids. I knew immediately this was the home for these two cuddly kitties. They were about to get more attention than I had given them in months and they deserved it.

Greg and I moved into a beautiful home that was pet-free and incredibly low-maintenance. I can hardly believe how easy life became. You might think that this is how the story ends, but have I mentioned that when you find yourself chasing after Jesus, He leads you to some of the craziest places? You won't even believe where life has taken me since our wedding on July 3, 2009.

I'll Follow Jesus...
Anywhere?

A month or two before our wedding, my mom told me over the phone, "Did you know your cousin is in jail in Sarnia?" Of course, I knew she was referring to my cousin Tom, my dad's sister's son.

I didn't really know Tom. My grandma used to hold a family reunion once a year and that was about the only time I saw anyone on my dad's side of the family. Grandma passed away when I was in Grade Four, so I would have been in Grade Three (about seven or eight years old) the last time I saw any of them. Tom was five years older than I was, so he would have been a teenager and certainly not hanging out with me at these reunions. I knew what he generally looked like, but he was basically a complete stranger to me.

One thing I knew about Tom was that his dad was a good man who had passed away when Tom was quite young. He had two older brothers and two older sisters. I'd heard that his one brother had been a great guy, a hard worker, and much like his dad, but he, too, died young. The other brother had fallen hard into alcohol and I wasn't sure about his sisters. I thought they were all quite a bit older than him, though, and had moved out or were about to move out of the family home when he was still young. His mom may have met and dated different men over the years and I wasn't sure how any of them had treated Tom.

Another thing I knew was that Tom and a buddy had gotten the bright idea one day that they should try to rob a bank. They did, and then robbed one in the United States as well before getting caught and thrown into prison there. He spent several years in prison before being transferred back to Canada and spending ten years of his life in Kingston Penitentiary. Tom was bad news. Any time his name came up in conversation, it was because someone was asking if he was out of jail yet, or back in it.

That's all that I knew about Tom.

I asked what he was in jail for this time.

"Murder," my mom said.

What? I understood that his life was hard and he had made some awful decisions that took him to dreadful places, but murder? How had it all come to this? My mom was surprised that I hadn't at least heard about it on the radio or in the paper. There was no body and no real evidence, just the testimony of his sister claiming he had told her he did it, and his testimony that she was lying.

I went to bed that night feeling very sad. For some strange reason, hearing about this was no different than hearing about a murder case on the news; I didn't know the people involved and it really didn't affect my life in any way. Still, I couldn't shake my intense sadness for this woman who had gone missing and was presumed dead, for her family who must be grieving so terribly and still getting no real closure, for Tom who'd had good parents who would have wanted a great life for him, and yet the early death of his father had caused everything to spin out of control. It all just made me sad.

I woke up the next morning feeling as though I was having a heart attack. It was like a house rested on my chest. I could barely breathe. At the same time, I felt as though I was being told I had to visit Tom. I thought this was ridiculous, so I fought the notion. Really? I had to visit Tom in jail? I didn't even know him! He had no idea who I was! What would it matter to him if I showed up to say hi or not? He would probably just tell me off and scream at me to leave. I came up with every logical reason I could think of to not visit him (and there were many).

What I got in return was this:

> Religion that God our Father ac-
> cepts as pure and faultless is this:
> to look after orphans and widows
> in their distress and to keep one-
> self from being polluted by the
> world. (James 1:27)

Then this:

> He upholds the cause of the op-
> pressed and gives food to the hun-
> gry. The Lord sets prisoners free.
> (Psalm 146:7)

I was reminded that I was a widow, and He had sent people to do their best to take care of me. He was asking no more of me than to do the same for a prisoner. Being in jail didn't make Tom less a child of God. I knew what I was being told to do and I intended to do it, but I was completely and utterly terrified.

I contacted a friend of mine who was a police officer (who knew and loved God and also might be able to understand where I was being led). I asked how I would go about visiting Tom in jail. He gave me the phone number I needed to make an appointment and explained that they would tell me the times I could visit and how often. Beyond that, all I had to do was show up. The ball was placed back in my hands.

Time passed quickly, though, and our wedding was less than a month away. I became consumed with wedding preparations, then the honeymoon, and then moving into our new home. Soon, Tom dropped right off my radar. Not for long. Out of the blue, as I was jogging before work one morning, God told me that He hadn't for-gotten. I still needed to visit Tom.

By this time, I had joined a new small group. We were a crazy mix of people who were dealing with everything from losing a hus-band to alcoholism, drug abuse to depression. We were a motley crew and this was one of the realest, rawest small groups I had ever been a part of. We studied His Word because we *needed* it, not be-cause we felt we should. We felt free to share anything about our lives because we just knew someone else had either gone through the same or dealt with much worse. There was no fear of judgement. I explained to them that I felt as though I was being told to visit Tom in jail. Then I burst into tears. I shook from crying so hard. Mike, who led our small group, pulled me aside afterward and asked where the intense emotion was coming from. I explained that I felt terrified because God had very clearly told me to go, but He hadn't told me what to say. What could I possibly say? I felt ill-prepared and fully expected this hardened criminal to leer at me and make me feel like a fool for showing up at all.

Mike suggested that this may be something worth fasting and praying over, that maybe I was being told to go but I didn't necessarily have to be the one to be in constant communication with him. He even told me that he felt comfortable visiting inmates and if it got too awkward, I could just tell Tom that I knew someone who would be happy to visit him if he'd like. This helped and I went home feeling better.

My appointment was set for the next afternoon. I went for a five-kilometre jog that morning. For the first half, I prayed constantly, asking God to give me the words and confidence to know what to do. Then it occurred to me that it might be wise to actually be quiet so I could hear if He was trying to speak to me. I ran in silence for the last half and every little sound a bird made, or a leaf rustling on the street, had me wondering if there was meaning in it.

I turned the last corner toward my house and started to feel angry. Nothing. He had given me nothing. Had He not heard the desperation with which I was praying? I was about to make myself breakfast when I recalled what Mike had said about it being worth fasting over. I passed on breakfast and decided instead to use that time to read the Bible. Maybe something in there would jump out at me. I randomly opened it and began to read.

It wasn't long before I came across 1 Corinthians 1:26–31, which says,

> Brothers [and sisters], think of what you were when you were called. Not many of you were wise by human standards; not many were influential; not many were of noble birth. But God chose the foolish things of the world

to shame the wise; God chose the weak things of the world to shame the strong. He chose the lowly things of this world and the despised things—and the things that are not—to nullify the things that are, so that no one may boast before him. It is because of him that you are in Christ Jesus, who has become for us wisdom from God—that is, our righteousness, holiness and redemption. Therefore, as it is written: "Let the one who boasts boast in the Lord."

And there it was. That was exactly the message God wanted me to share with Tom. He may have been considered low and despised in this world, but God was going to use him in mighty ways, and in doing so, the only one who would be glorified was God. Tom's life was about to change, and he didn't even know it yet.

When Paths Cross
Lives Are Changed

I printed off this verse, tucked it in my pocket, then made my way to the jail. I had never been there and didn't really know where to go, so I stopped at the police station along the way to ask for directions.

Once at the station, the officer behind the front desk was very pleasant and asked how he could help me. I explained that I was heading to the jail but wasn't sure where to go or what to do when I got there. He asked who I was visiting and when I said Tom's name, he asked, "Why are you visiting him?" His face turned from a pleasant expression to one of complete disgust.

"Good question," I replied. "He's my cousin."

He composed himself and explained which door I needed to go to and that I would be buzzed in from there.

As I continued on my way, I felt ill wondering just how badly Tom was being treated. If the mere mention of his name could make a grown man turn instantly into a hateful little boy, how much different would it be for him within the walls of the prison? I got buzzed in and was immediately intimidated. You cannot see behind the two-way mirror to know who you're speaking with. They speak in clipped tones and are very no-nonsense. They slide a tray out and tell you to put your identification in it. You wait until they tell you to enter and then they buzz you into the visitation room.

It's just like you see on television. There was a row of stools and a phone to pick up. Glass separated me from the prisoners. Tom was brought in and I was surprised to realize that there was something about his appearance that was familiar to me, even though it had been more than twenty years since I had seen him. He looked at me curiously, not knowing who I was. I think he believed I was there on behalf of his lawyer.

"You don't know me, do you?" I asked.

He said he didn't.

"The truth is, I don't know you either. Do you know who Doug is?"

"Sure," he said. "I know Uncle Doug."

"I'm his youngest daughter, Jennifer."

He couldn't believe it and said the last time he'd seen me I was probably about knee-high.

"Tom, it's sort of weird how I came to be here," I replied, "but I need to share something with you."

He told me to go ahead. I explained about how my mom had told me he was in prison and then a little about his life growing up. When I mentioned his mom, he looked down.

"Yeah, that's my fault," he said.

I had no idea what he was referring to, but I did know that his mom had passed away while he was in Sarnia prison waiting for sentencing. Her funeral had been the day after my wedding and I'd been unable to attend.

"She was so stressed over my being in here," he said. "It killed her."

I told him I was sure that wasn't true, but he couldn't look at me after that. I wasn't going to let him off the hook that easily. I insisted that he look me in the eyes.

"That's not true," I said. "If anything, she would have wanted to fight to live longer so she could be here for you. She died because it was her time and that's all there is to it. You have to stop telling yourself these lies. They'll eat you up inside."

He said he'd try, and then I continued on with the reason for my visit. I told him that if there was one thing he should know about me, it was that I was prayerful. I'd had a great life, then I had lost my husband to cancer, and now I was starting yet another great life—and it was only by the grace of God.

Tom nodded.

"Tom, I felt as though I was being told to visit you, but I didn't know why," I continued. "Why would you want to see me? We don't even know each other. I stressed over this for quite a while and prayed about it a lot. Then I came across this." I held up the folded piece of paper I had brought along. "May I read it to you?" He said I could and I read the passage from 1 Corinthians 1:26–31, beginning to cry as I did so.

"I don't know if this makes sense to you yet, but it will," I said between tears. "I believe God told me to come see you to let you know that He isn't finished with you yet. He has great plans for you, and it doesn't matter where you are, even in jail. He can do great works in you and through you. Basically what I'm saying is, God's calling, and you're up."

I told him it was okay if he thought I was crazy, but he said he didn't. He was thankful that I had taken the time to see him and share this with him. He told me that he didn't want to be a bother to me and he certainly didn't expect me to visit anymore, but he could always use a pen pal, if I ever felt like writing him.

On my drive home, I felt so much lighter for having obeyed God. Tom had been so much nicer to me than I would have ever imagined. I had no real intentions of visiting him again, though. God had said go, I'd gone, and now my part was done. Even Tom had said I didn't have to go back again.

I hadn't even made it halfway home when I heard a very clear voice say, *"You need to go back."*

God! Really? What would we talk about this time?

I didn't know, but I knew I could do it. It wouldn't be as traumatic as I had initially thought it would be, so I booked another visitation. A week later, I was back again and I knew what I needed to say. He smiled at me when he was led in and saw me sitting there.

"You are one crazy brave girl, you know that?" he asked.

Crazy stupid was more like it, but at least we could both agree I was crazy. I told him I had been thinking about him and there was something else I needed to share. I explained that after Clarence had died, I'd blamed myself. There were always new reports coming out saying things like "microwaving your food causes cancer" or "this plant cures cancer" and I would think that if only I had been a better cook, we wouldn't have had to microwave so many meals, and if only I had done more research, I might have heard about this plant in time, and so on. These thoughts tore me apart!

It took a long time for me to remember that God knows the very second we will be born, and He knows the moment we will take our last breath. Clarence was going to die on January 25, 2007 whether I cooked with a microwave or not. Because I hadn't told anyone about these crazy thoughts, I suffered silently for months—until God gently told me otherwise. Had I shared some of my crazier thoughts with someone, they may have been able to help me to understand that I was wrong, sparing me a lot of heartache.

Tom didn't have that, either. He didn't have anyone he could share his craziest thoughts with. Had I not shown up and heard him say that he believed he killed his own mother, he would have gone on believing that for who knows how long? I told him I wasn't going anywhere. I was going to start visiting him whenever I could, and I would write as well... and I demanded that he be honest with me when sharing his thoughts so that I could help him determine if they were based in truth or not. He said he would try and we began to chat. I told him about my life in a nutshell and he told me about his. I had to admit, when I'd heard he fled to the U.S. and robbed a bank, I thought that was funny (in a ridiculous sort of way). Who really does that? He laughed and said it sort of cracked him up, too, that he actually thought he could get away with it.

As we became more comfortable with each other, we shared more and more about our lives. He swore that he hadn't committed murder, and to be honest it didn't matter to me. I don't believe God led me to Tom to judge him; He led me there to *love* him. Could Tom have done it? Sure, absolutely. Couldn't any of us, really? The story is that he was in a heated argument with his girlfriend when he grabbed her hair from behind and yanked her around, breaking her neck in the process. He then buried the body and it has yet to be found. He denies every part of this, but even if it were one hundred percent true, don't we all have that in us? We like to think we don't, that only animals behave that way, but we are all attracted to some area of darkness. Some of us are able to manage it, but others aren't so fortunate.

I have a very addictive personality. That's the trait in me that says, "I think I'm going to start running," and then in a very short time I find myself running a half-marathon without being even close to prepared. I have no off-button once I press start. I could have written a journal, but instead I dove right in and wrote a book. I'm fortunate that I haven't taken up drinking, because I have no doubt I would quickly spiral out of control.

While I may have these traits under control, for the most part, a part of me still thinks I can have just a small dish of ice cream and then shudders when thirty minutes later I find myself licking out an empty box. I still struggle with food and I imagine I always will. I can say that I would never kill anyone, that this is a line I would never cross, but when Clarence was weak and dying, had someone hurt him, I wouldn't have thought twice about attacking that person with deadly force. People might justify it and think, "Well, that's different, you were protecting someone," but the fact remains that if the conditions were right and you found yourself in a perfect storm, if you were being completely honest with yourself, you would have to admit that even you could be capable of doing unthinkable things.

So then, is it possible that Tom committed this crime? Sure it is. Do I think he did it? Not really. I think he had a lawyer who was caught up with a higher profile case and gave him little time or energy. I think she failed to ask some important questions and was ineffective at getting deeper answers. His representation was lacking at best, his history haunted him, and it wasn't hard to look at such a large man and see someone who could break the neck of a tiny woman. I think Tom was failed by the justice system; while he's very much guilty of making awful decisions in his life, that alone doesn't make him a murderer.

He is currently in Kingston Penitentiary serving a life sentence with no chance for parole for seventeen years. I don't feel entirely bad for him, though. The truth is, I'm even a little excited for him. To understand that, you need to know some of the crazier things that have happened while he was in jail in Sarnia. First, I was prompted to visit him while he was still a stranger to me. Then the jail became grossly overcrowded and they ended up giving him a cellmate. This cellmate was in for things much tamer than murder and I'm sure he was terrified to find out who he'd be rooming with. Oh, and one more thing: this cellmate was a Christian.

I explained to Tom that I wasn't there to judge or condemn him; I was there to walk with him. In the meantime, Tom's cellmate was talking to him about his own faith and the bizarre circumstances that had landed him in prison. He constantly received letters from members of his church back home (he was from the United States) and they never stopped reminding him that he was in their thoughts and prayers, that they were doing everything possible to get him out of jail. Tom was seeing what God-loving, God-fearing people look like: love, forgiveness, and faithfulness. He was intrigued by it all. Then, a couple of guys decided to pass the time by taking some courses—Bible courses, no less! Tom overheard them discussing verses and arguing over what they might mean.

One day, Tom's name was called because he had a visitor. He didn't know who it was, but it turned out to be a pastor who on occasion did random visits with random prisoners, and on this day he chose Tom.

These may seem like small things individually, but when you add them up, they become too big to be coincidental. I knew it, Tom's cellmate knew it, and he was slowly starting to see it as well. He decided to sign up for those Bible courses and he dove right into them. When he completed a section, he was given a certificate with his grade and a new booklet to work through. He mailed those certificates to me for safekeeping.

When at home, I often set my Bible on the kitchen counter. I had decided in 2008 that I was going to read the Bible from cover to cover in a year. I was tired of knowing small bits and pieces of what was in the Bible, but not knowing the whole story. It felt important to know the Bible for myself, so I wouldn't just believe what other people told me. I'm glad I did that.

I happen to have an awful memory when it comes to detail, but I remember the broader things. At times I've heard "truths" from the Bible only to have a sense that they were different from what I had read. I would flip through the Bible until I found what I was looking for, to see if I was being told the whole truth or not. If you haven't read the Bible but think you know what it's about, I highly recommend that you don't simply take someone else's word for it, even if they sound knowledgeable. We do research before we buy a car or a home to make sure we don't get duped, so shouldn't it be just as important to understand our eternity?

I wasn't successful in reading the entire Bible in a year; it took me exactly two years. During those two years, I cannot tell you how many times I read something just as I needed it. I would tell a small lie and then read that night before bed that God hates lies.

> There are six things which the Lord hates,
>   Yes, seven which are an abomination to Him:
>   Haughty eyes, a lying tongue,
>   And hands that shed innocent blood,
>   A heart that devises wicked plans,

Feet that run rapidly to evil,
A false witness who utters lies,
And one who spreads strife among
brothers. (Proverbs 6:16–19, NASB)

Sometimes, even after being married to Greg, I would feel lonely. One time, I came across this:

God sets the lonely in families,
he leads forth the prisoners with
singing; but the rebellious live in
a sun-scorched land. (Psalm 68:6)

I realized then that I wasn't lonely, not really. I had been placed in a wonderful family and given an incredible husband. Instead of wallowing in self-pity, I decided that since I now knew what loneliness looked like and how it felt, I should probably do something about it. Since then, I've made a point of starting conversations with people who appear to be alone. I can vouch that while being lonely is difficult, feeling lonely in a crowd is the worst. I try not to let anyone go unnoticed in a crowd, if I can help it. I've met some great people that way and look forward to meeting many more. It occurred to me that while I would hang back and wait for someone to strike up a conversation with me, what if they were doing the same thing? Someone has to be the first to step out of their comfort zone. What makes me so special that I should assume it will always be their job and never mine?

I've had too many great experiences to count from reading the Bible. I've been corrected, encouraged, lifted up, loved, and forgiven. It's probably the greatest book of all time and somehow we make every excuse under the sun not to read it. If you haven't read it yet, I highly recommend it!

The only problem with this Bible of mine was that it was a gift from Clarence's mom and it had "Clarence and Jen Lenting" written on the front in gold letters. I felt as though every time Greg walked by it, he was reminded that he was my second husband. He never complained about it and never would, but one day I saw him glance at it, then look away. I felt in my heart that it was time to get a new

Bible. I'd been meaning to buy one but just wasn't able to get to the store in time.

A few weeks went by. I picked up our mail from the post office one day and found a note telling me that I had a parcel waiting. That was odd, since I hadn't ordered anything. When I opened the package, I reached in and pulled out... a white Bible! I didn't know how or why, but I thought this was one of the coolest things God ever did for me.

It got better. I pulled it all the way out of the packaging and, in gold letters along the front, it said "Jen Dawson." Who had done this? I hadn't told anyone about my desire for a new Bible. How could this be? On the inside was a small note stating that the Bible had been for Tom and that he had asked that it be sent to me. Once he had completed all his courses, he was eligible to get a free Bible with his name embossed, but because he couldn't bring in books from outside the jail, they said he could send it to anyone he wished and have their name printed on it instead. Without even knowing he had done it, Tom was used by God to answer one of my prayers. How cool is that?

I then received an amazing letter from Tom. In November 2009, he wrote me to let me know that on Remembrance Day he had finally "gotten it" and he could deny the existence of God no more. He had accepted Jesus Christ into his life as his Lord and Saviour. He was saved!

In the months leading up to this, there was a little bit of tension between Greg and me. He didn't care to hear about my visits with Tom, he had no desire whatsoever to read any of the letters, and sometimes he seemed a little standoffish when I mentioned Tom in conversation. This began to bother me because the easy solution was for me to stop writing and visiting Tom. The only problem was that I wasn't the one who had decided to do this. In fact, I had pushed against it and tried not to visit him for months. I knew in my heart that this was something God wanted me to do, and if God was leading, then I had to follow. Since I had no intention of going against God, that meant Greg would have to change in some way. I prayed and prayed that he would have a change of heart and open up to the idea of me having a relationship with Tom. Nothing seemed to change and I didn't know what else to do. If God wasn't going to change Greg's heart, I certainly wouldn't be able to.

I went to work and even read Tom's letter to my coworkers. They thought it was very cool and I could barely contain my joy. As the day came to an end, I thought about going home and how

I wouldn't be able to share this great news with Greg because he wouldn't care. It would just burst my bubble, which made me a little sad. I figured I just wouldn't tell Greg. Then, over dinner, I thought to myself, *I have to tell Greg. He's my husband and this is important to me. My husband should know everything important about me. If I don't tell him, my coworkers will know more about this part of my life than him and eventually that will only make me bitter and cause a wedge.*

After dinner, Greg sat in the living room. I asked if he would do me a favour. He said yes and I asked him if he would please read Tom's latest letter. He agreed and I waited nervously, hoping that his response wouldn't crush me.

When he finished reading it, he looked at me. "Tom's saved?"

"It seems so."

"Jen! Tom's saved! This is *huge!* Can I pray about this?"

I was surprised at how enthusiastic Greg was. "That would be great."

Greg prayed for Tom and his continued walk with the Lord. He thanked God for having me visit Tom, and then he prayed for God to call him to do something in a similarly meaningful way.

Then it all made sense. Greg hadn't been upset about my relationship with Tom; he had seen this cool thing God was doing with me and he wanted to experience it, too. In that one day, I received news that my cousin had gone from sinner and imprisoned to saved and set free, *and* I had the honour of listening in on my husband's prayer in which he asked God to walk him through something equally exciting.

The crazy thing about prayer is, be careful what you pray for because God doesn't tend to do things halfway. I don't think Greg or I knew what we were in for.

When God Takes Prayers Literally

One thing I truly respect about Greg is the way he handles money. He's the farthest thing from materialistic you could possibly get. He rarely buys new clothes; he just takes really good care of the clothes he has, and he always looks great. He drives a 2001 Chevy Malibu that he refers to as "Malibu Stacie." He bought it off his parents when they were done with it. He has no desire to get a newer, flashier car unless his should die, and even then he talks about which used vehicle he would likely purchase. He doesn't spend much money on himself, and when he does he feels guilty about it. He is very generous and has no problem giving to others. He pays his bills, then saves the rest.

I think I'm alright with how I handle money, but I aspire to be as mature with it as Greg is. I had no problem considering "my" money "our" money when we got married because I knew it would be handled responsibly. I use the term "my" loosely, though, because I'm very aware that what I have—all of it—is God's. He has blessed us with a nice home and two vehicles that run. We're able to take vacations and not stress over the cost of groceries. We're grateful for all of it and do our best to use it wisely. Also, we're very aware that as nice as it is to have these things, God can take any or all of it back at any point in time—and that's okay, too. It was never ours to begin with.

We claimed to both feel that way, but God was about to put us to the test.

A good friend of mine, Pat, cleans houses and once every other week she cleaned ours. One week, Greg and I both got a bonus from work at the same time. Basically, we got paycheques that were double their normal size. Pat was coming over to clean that week and I thought it would be nice to give her a bonus, too. We were realizing how good it felt, so why not share the feeling?

I'm weird about money and tend to like to deal in even numbers. I'll pump gas to an even fifty cents or round up to the next dollar, but paying $38.93 for gas would make me crazy. We normally paid Pat sixty dollars, so I thought I would give her an even hundred. I had written out the cheque and then got in the shower to start getting ready for work. While in the shower (I don't know why I tend to hear from God in the shower most often, but maybe it's because I'm the most relaxed there), I heard this: *"You both got double your pay."*

I instantly felt embarrassed for nearly ripping Pat off. When I got out of the shower, I tore up the cheque and wrote a new one for $120. She showed up before I left for work and I explained what had happened. I apologized for almost short-changing her, but she said she was glad it had happened that way because now we knew it was from God, and not just me trying to throw extra money at her. I agreed. I prefer doing nice things when God leads as opposed to doing them on my own and then feeling as though I did something special and getting prideful about it. Both Pat and I praised God for the way He was working in our lives. I then headed to work.

I was attending a Wednesday night small group and my friend Nicole and I had started to go out for a coffee on occasion afterwards (and by coffee, I mean steamed milk). We did this a few weeks in a row. Each time before we parted ways, she asked me to please pray for Pat because she sensed Pat wasn't doing very well. I said that I would and I usually did throw out a quick prayer, but at that time Pat was more on Nicole's radar than mine. I was very much caught up in writing to and praying for Tom.

Again, the next week Nicole asked me to pray for Pat and I agreed to. I wasn't exactly sure what Nicole was referring to. I knew Pat had battled cancer quite a few years ago and since having chemotherapy and radiation, she sometimes felt ill now. I prayed for continued health and strength through any rough times as they may come up. Yet again, Nicole asked me to please, please keep Pat in my thoughts and prayers. I assured her that I would.

One day I was driving home from work when a horrible feeling came over me. Greg and I had a good-sized savings account and I suddenly thought, *What if we were to both die? How would I ever explain the fact that we were just sitting on all this money?* It started to really bother me and I asked God to help me determine what to do with it. I sensed that "sit on it until you retire" wasn't where He was leading us. A few days went by and this feeling became a little more frantic, but I still didn't know what we were supposed to do.

Nicole and I sometimes emailed back and forth. In her email, she asked me for the hundredth time to please pray for Pat. It took a while, but I suddenly realized what was going on. God was placing Pat before me repeatedly while prompting me to do something with this money. Now it made sense.

"Okay, God, I get it," I said. "You want Pat to have some of this money. No problem. It's your money, we can move it wherever you want. I just need you to tell me how much."

I had been burned once before. A girl I knew once told me a sad story and, since I'm a total bleeding heart, I instantly wanted to help. I gave her a fair bit of money. She had been thrilled with my generosity and I hadn't minded doing it for her. What I did mind came a few months later, when we were sitting outside chatting and she made a comment about how she knew how to work people and she could get anything she wanted simply by asking the right way. She was almost bragging about how smart she was, but I couldn't help but think she was anything but for two reasons. First, I would have gladly helped her on other occasions after that, but realized that she was just using me, so she never received another dime from me. Second, how smart was it to give away her game plan? She did me a big favour, though, because I realized then that I would never give away money just because someone had a heart-breaking story. Most of us do. I only offer help financially when God presents a need to me and then very specifically tells me how He wants me to meet that need.

I now felt as though God had shown me an area of need, regarding Pat, but I had no intention of doing anything until He told me how much to give. Before you swoop in and save the day for someone financially, remember that being able to give is actually a blessing. It's a blessing to be able to help others. If someone needs a thousand dollars and you swoop in and play the hero, that person will feel blessed for having had their need met and you'll feel blessed for having been able to meet the need. The problem is, if ten people were all willing and able to give a hundred dollars, then you stole an opportunity for nine others to experience that blessing. I've learned that God is amazing at meeting people's needs, but His ways aren't our ways and His thoughts aren't our thoughts. That's why it's so important to get your direction from Him first—but once you do, be ready to move.

For days, I prayed about how much to give and I began to feel frustrated. One morning as I was getting ready for work, I hopped into the shower and said out loud, "I don't understand, God. You clearly want us to give Pat money to meet a need of hers, but you won't tell me how much. What do we do with that?"

Before I got out of the shower, I heard, *"I didn't give you an amount because that's my answer. Give her as much as she needs."*

My knees nearly buckled. What was "as much as she needs"? What if she needed more than we had? What if her need required us to sell a vehicle, or our home, to be able to meet it? This felt like a lot to be asked, but after recovering from the initial shock, I realized what He was saying: *"If she needs it, give it to her. Haven't I taken great care of you? Is she any less important? Is it better for you to have and her not to have than for her to have and you to go without?"*

Of course He was right, and again, the money wasn't mine to hold on to. Here's the thing: up until this point, I hadn't mentioned any of this to Greg. We shared everything, including our money, but we also allowed each other a certain amount of "free" money that was ours to spend without having to answer to the other person. We always told each other if we made any sort of large purchase, out of respect and so the other person was aware of what was going on, but if I wanted to throw someone a hundred dollars, Greg wouldn't mind in the least, and vice versa. I realized now, though, that we weren't talking about a hundred dollars; this could be more than either of us had bargained for. I needed to talk to him quickly.

That night over supper, I explained the whole situation and how I had felt that Pat had been laid on my heart and we were to give her as much money as she needed.

"What does that mean?" Greg asked.

"Exactly that. As much as she needs."

I asked him to take some time to pray about this, and I would do the same. We'd then talk about it in a couple of days to see if we were on the same page. Greg agreed, and that was the end of the discussion.

A couple of days later, I still strongly felt that we were to give her as much as she needed. I asked Greg if he had been praying about it and he said he had. I asked if he was feeling led in any certain direction and he said, "I believe we should give her in the low twenties." I asked again if he had prayed about that number and he said that he had, that he felt strongly about this. I said that was fine and we decided to invite Pat over for dinner.

I have to admit, I was very disappointed with Greg. I knew in my heart that we were supposed to give her whatever she needed and I was disappointed that Greg would claim to have prayed about it, then put a cap on the dollar amount. He was my husband, though, and I valued his opinion. He had never led us astray and I trusted the way he led our home, so I agreed to abide by his decision.

When I woke up the next morning, and while I was getting ready for work, I prayed about this one last time. I knew time was short since Pat was coming over for dinner, so I asked God to let me know one last time that what we were doing was good, and okay, and most importantly that it was what He wanted and not just what we wanted. I needed to know that we were doing this according to His plan and not somehow interfering with His plan.

I grabbed a cheque and filled out Pat's name and mine, then put it in my purse. I left the dollar amount blank. I left for work, but before going there, I picked up the mail—something I hadn't done for a few days. What was there? A letter from my cousin Tom. It said:

> We write a blank cheque only for those we trust. We sign and hand it over with the words "You fill in the date and amount. I trust you implicitly." Will we give God that right in our own lives? Will we seek His will, determined to at all costs, and once it is known do it?

How crazy was that?! Not only that, but he finished his letter by describing a book called *The Screwtape Letters*, by C.S. Lewis, and insisting that I read it. I had only heard of this book twice before in my life. Both times it had been raved about —and both times by Pat. I knew that this letter was about Pat and telling me that, yes, this was God's will for her. I could trust Him in proceeding with this.

The three of us had a nice dinner together and then Greg made an excuse to leave so that Pat and I could talk. In the middle of the conversation, I asked her if I could ask a very personal question, assuring her that she didn't have to answer it.

"Sure," she said.

"Pat, how much money are you in debt?"

She had no problem answering and wasn't embarrassed about it. While she had undergone treatments for cancer, she was unable to work, so she literally lived off credit cards. Everything she had bought from groceries to paying bills, etc., was on credit. She said she had about seventeen thousand dollars in debt on her credit cards.

"Oh, and I haven't had a dime to be able to pay taxes for the past few years, so I haven't," she added. "I owe about five thousand in taxes."

"Aside from house payments, which are normal, if you paid off these things, would you be debt free?"

Pat said she would be.

I started to cry. I wanted so desperately to be faithful in how I followed Him and I was willing to give her anything we had. Greg had sworn he prayed about it and he kept sensing that we should give her in the low twenties. Twenty-two thousand was exactly how much Pat was in debt. I *was* being faithful, and so was Greg! He was very faithfully leading this household and obeying God's direction. It was exciting to have God show us that we were both being faithful, and that when we do that we ultimately end up on the same page.

I asked her if she would accept a cheque from us for $23,500 to pay off her debt and get her on the right track again.

Now Pat started to cry. I explained how all of this had come from Nicole's constant prayer requests, my own uneasiness, and then our being led to find the right amount. I even told her about Tom's letter, confirming that this was what God wanted us to do. All these things had led us to want to do this.

Pat thanked us and said that if we didn't mind, she would like to pray before accepting the money. We said that was fine and she headed home. I carried that cheque around in my purse until I saw her again. I couldn't believe that God would put us through all that, just to have her say she didn't want it. I understand how humbling it can be to receive gifts from others, but this money wasn't ours and He wanted her to have it, of that I was sure.

A few days later, I saw her at small group. I approached her afterward to ask if she had prayed about it. She said that for the past two days all she could think about was being able to tithe this money, to give the first ten percent back to God. She was excited at the thought of giving money to Him to see how He would use it. Then He gently reminded her, *"You can't tithe it if you don't accept it."* With that, she accepted.

We asked her not to tell anyone. We didn't want it to be about us and what we had done, and we also didn't want people crawling out of the woodwork looking for money. She agreed to this, but did tell her father, who was a pastor, and asked that they keep it between them. He was excited for Pat and to see how God was so obviously working in all our lives. He commented that it was great to see Christians who owned their money without their money owning them.

The reason I'm writing about this now is because it's time. All these "God stories" have been adding up and I felt it was time to let others in, to show people how amazing He is. Pat once mentioned that she was disappointed she couldn't tell anyone because this was the coolest God story ever. She was excited when I asked her if I could include it. I have a feeling she'll be first in line to read this book.

Mirrors Show Reflections, God Reveals Self

My walk with God hasn't been all fun and games. He's had me do some crazy things that made me more than a little nervous, but He has also been working on me a great deal these past few years.

One morning, I did something I had never done before. I got down on my knees and put my face to the ground in a posture of complete submission. I prayed that God would show me who I really am—all of it, the good and the bad—and then help me to become the person He wants me to be. I had no idea what I had just done. I didn't realize that sometimes before you can get a person to be great, you have to break them into tiny pieces first. I spent months being repeatedly broken as He walked me through one weakness after another. It turns out that having your "bad spots" revealed to you is intense. One of the most difficult things a person will ever experience, in my opinion.

The first year of marriage for Greg and I was good, but unsteady. I take full blame for that. My moods were unpredictable. He never quite knew what he was going to come home to. That had a big effect on him, and ultimately on our marriage. Greg's schedule remained busy and he was always visiting with this friend or that. I began to feel as though I had seen him more when we were dating than when we were married. When he did stay home, it felt as though he was only doing it to appease me, not because he wanted to hang out with me. On those nights, I wished he would go out and leave me alone.

I began to resent him, and his friends, too. I felt very much alone and almost betrayed by him. When I tried to talk to him about spending so much time away from home, he acted as though I was crazy and said that he spent plenty of time with me. The very next night, I came home to a note saying that he was watching the game at his friend's house. He came waltzing in around 2:00 a.m. In my mind, he might as well have written "I don't care about you" on that note.

By the time he got home, I hated him. I actually hated him. I couldn't imagine spending the rest of my life with him. I slept on the very edge of the bed so that I wouldn't have to feel his presence near me. I pretended to sleep so I wouldn't have to kiss him goodbye in the morning. I wondered whether I should pack my bags or his. I was done. I sent him an email from work saying that I finally understood. He wanted to be married; he just didn't want his life to change in any way, shape, or form.

"That's cool," I said. "Consider me a roommate, nothing more. Enjoy your life."

That was a rough night in the Dawson household. Things were very awkward between us and we had a long talk, both sharing our frustrations. To be honest, I don't fully remember what either of us said.

The big impact came the next day as I was driving home from work. A song called "How He Loves" began to play:

> He is jealous for me,
> Loves like a hurricane; I am a tree…

The song goes on, but that was enough. It occurred to me that God was jealous *for* me—not jealous *of* me. He wants nothing more than for us to know and love the One who knew and loved us first. He waits patiently while we worship everything from our finances to our jobs to our appearance to other people. He watches us do all those things, but He doesn't hate us or leave us. He waits patiently, because He loves us that much. He loved us first, and He wants us back. He is jealous for us.

I felt as though Greg didn't love me first and I was punishing him for it. The thing is, I *loved* Greg and if I truly wanted to love him the way God loves me, I needed to let him go. I even needed to encourage him to go, if these were the things that made him happy, because ultimately, wasn't that what I wanted, for Greg to be happy?

I decided that things needed to change, but those changes had to happen in me. I decided that I wasn't going to tell Greg about my revelation; I was just going to allow God to walk me through these changes. Hopefully, I would see the effect it had on Greg.

When I started to pay more attention to God, allowing Him to lead me in becoming the wife I should be, life became easier. The first thing I noticed was that when Greg walked in the front door, he would say "Hello?" in a timid voice. He was calling out to hear my reply and gauge what he was in for. He knew that if my reply was short and clipped, things weren't going to be fun, and if I seemed bubbly and happy, we would be okay. That made me incredibly sad. This was Greg's home! He should have been able to walk into it confidently; he may have had a rough day at work or be in a bad mood for whatever reason, but this should be the one place he knew he could go where everything was okay. Our home should have been a safe haven for both of us. I realized that I had done this to him. My sporadic moods had put him on edge so much that he practically tiptoed into the house. No wonder he could hardly wait to get out of it!

From that point on, I made it my mission to always greet him pleasantly—always. I also decided that not only would I not complain about his spending time with friends, I would encourage it. I used to enjoy spending time alone doing my own thing and there was no reason I couldn't get back to that place. I had made Greg my God and was counting on him to provide me comfort and happiness, but that had to stop. That was too much pressure for any one person. Once I put God back in His rightful place in my life and treated Greg as my husband and friend, everything changed for the better. Instead of being angry when he got home, I would ask how his night went and give positive feedback as he told me about it. It took a while and at first I'm sure he thought I was setting him up.

Slowly but surely, I watched him start to come bounding in the front door and yell out "Hello!" full volume. He would come find me wherever I was in the house and we would chat about our day and if we had any plans for the evening. If one or both of us had made plans of our own, we would come together at the end of the night and compare notes.

Sometimes he now turns his friends down and I encourage him to go, but he says he really wants to be home with me. What a difference a year has made! I love seeing him walk around our house with confidence. I love that he knows I'm his biggest supporter and not his biggest headache. In turn, he takes such great care of me! Greg cooks more than ninety percent of our meals, he cleans, he plays games with me, and he shares the details of his day with me. In return, I take care of him every chance I get because some days I feel so pampered that it almost feels wrong.

We have worked through so much. I swear that when you walk into our home, you can feel that the atmosphere is light and the house is filled with love. I'm so glad I hadn't confided how I'd been feeling a year ago to a girlfriend, because girls tend to want to support each other and I'm sure I would have been told that he was a jerk, that I was in the right. Likewise, had Greg run to his friends, they would have assured him that I was crazy and that's just the way women are, that he would be better off staying away from home as much as possible. The great thing about taking your stuff to God is that He always tells you the truth in the gentlest way possible. The truth was that I was offside. Greg had reacted accordingly.

I can't imagine my life without him now. I'm not saying that in an unhealthy or unbalanced way. Greg isn't mine; he's God's, and should the time come that God wants him back, I'll respect that. I'll continue to be deeply and madly in love with my husband, now, and for as long as God allows.

Where He Leads,
I Will Follow

Then there was Remix. What's Remix, you ask? Remix is a missions trip of sorts that takes place in Toronto, Ontario. As youth leaders, we take students there for a week of learning about God and all the ways He loves us. Then we spend the afternoons putting those principles into practice with strangers on the street. I had taken the teens on weekend getaways before and they always made me nervous. I felt out of my league being called a "leader" and worried that not only would I answer a question wrong, but what if I said something that sent a teenager down the wrong path altogether? I take leadership very seriously and would never want to do it badly.

I was never the only leader on weekend trips, so I could rely heavily on others if I didn't have the answers. In June 2010, I joined Dave, the youth pastor at Temple Baptist Church, to take a group of fourteen teens to Toronto. There were eight boys and six girls. I figured Dave would handle the boys and I the girls. Upon arrival, I realized that Dave was very heavily involved in the operations of this event, and for the majority of the time I was the go-to leader. Had I only known the drama that would ensue, and just as much from the boys as the girls! I had never felt stretched so thin before, nor had I prayed so continually about every little thing. If you haven't noticed yet, I believe very much in the power of prayer. God and I have an ongoing conversation. I chat with Him often and not always to pray for things; sometimes I pray just to thank Him for being so amazing. Sometimes I pray to ask Him not to give up on me because I know I'm not there yet. Sometimes I literally pray to just say hi.

I felt like I was in over my head, but He walked me through each situation as it arose. On this trip, I met Bethany, a youth pastor at Bluewater Baptist Church in Sarnia. Bethany was a Godsend. One night, we had a chance to go out for dinner, just the two of us. We got to know each other well in a short amount of time. I knew immediately that she was someone I wanted in my life as a friend and for spiritual support. Her faith was real, transparent, and everything just made sense when she explained it to you.

One night, Bethany and I agreed to meet outside our rooms and head down to dinner together. I fell asleep and was basically comatose. I didn't hear my alarm at all. She was standing outside my door when some boys from Temple approached her and started to tell her about a conflict they were having. She calmed the situation down and dealt with it beautifully. I didn't know this until I finally woke up and rushed downstairs to join the group. Bethany filled me in on what had happened and what she had done. I was furious. These were *my* teens. I had been terrified to lead, but I was finally doing it and God was walking me through. Who was she to come along and just take over like that?

I said none of this to her, but I was secretly very annoyed. This feeling lasted until I got into my room and went to bed later that night. I lay there, fuming, until it occurred to me what she had said to the teens. I know for a fact that I wouldn't have dealt with the situation well; I would have been overly tired and snapped at them, brushing off their issues as silly and telling them to "get over it." I know I would have. I was in no frame of mind to handle the situation rationally.

That's when I learned a very important lesson; God won't give us anything we can't handle. Knowing this, I now jump when He says to move. I may not always feel confident, but I know He wouldn't ask if He knew I couldn't handle it. He placed Bethany in that hallway because those teens really did need some guidance, and she was equipped to give it to them. Once again I was humbled, left in awe of His ways.

The first night at Remix, we were given a devotional and a book called *The One Thing You Can't Do in Heaven*. When I went to bed that night, I read a couple of chapters. If you don't know, the one thing you can't do in Heaven is witness to people—you don't need to; they all know God. It was a neat concept and explained why it's so important to share your faith while you can. Within the first couple of chapters, the author said that when you're witnessing to people, it's not uncommon to have someone ask, "Are you an angel?" That's because God will often put you in the path of someone who desperately needs to hear your message and they'll wonder how you knew they needed to hear this.

The next day, we learned how to "see like God." We walked around in the afternoon and all we were supposed to do was see the need in the city, praying for people. A large group of us were walking along with me at the end of the pack. We passed a man sitting on the front steps of a building and he looked like he was in rough shape. He had a black eye and had obviously received some stitches just below his eye. As I passed, I happened to notice him at the exact same time he looked at me.

"Are you okay?" I asked.

He motioned for me to walk over to him. I was nervous, because I had zero sense of direction and I didn't want to get separated from the group, but I figured I could run and catch up to them if I didn't take too long.

"Are you with the government?" he asked.

I knew at this point that he was either supposed to be on medication that he wasn't taking, or he was on drugs of some sort and paranoid.

"No," I said. "Did you see that big group just walk by? Well, that's a group of teenagers from various churches. They've all come together in Toronto to learn about how God loves them, and then try to love others in that same way."

He started mumbling, but I could make out that he was reciting different Bible verses.

"It doesn't matter, though," he said. "It all comes down to love. It's just about love, that's all it is. Nobody loves me."

"No, that's just it," I said quickly. "That's why I'm here, to tell you that God loves you very much."

He got very still, looked me right in the eyes, and said, "What are you, an angel?"

I was so excited to have just read something and then experienced it immediately afterwards. I assured him that I wasn't an angel, but I knew God loved him. I asked if I could pray for him. He let me, and then he prayed for me!

151

Another day we learned about hearing as God hears, and that people just want to be heard. That afternoon, as we walked around the city, we came up to a stop light. A blind lady walked by with a white cane, calling out, "Hello? Could somebody help me?"

Dave and I were near her and we looked at each other, almost amused. It was as though God was placing one person after another in front of us to reinforce the lessons we had just learned.

I was closer to her, so I answered. "I'm here. May I help you?" She asked if I would mind helping her across the street. When the light turned green, we began to cross together. She talked the whole time. We got to the other side and I asked if she was alright.

"Actually, would you help me cross this next street?" she asked. "Then I know where I'm going."

I again said I would and we began to cross. Once again, she chatted quickly and animatedly the entire time. I couldn't help but notice how able she was with her cane. This lady knew every dip in the road like the back of her hand.

Once we crossed the second street, I explained that I had to get back to my friends, but I wished her well and thanked her for the conversation. As I ran to catch up with our group, I couldn't help but smile. This lady hadn't needed me or anyone else to help her cross the street. She merely needed a listening ear and a chance to have a little conversation. At the end of the day, isn't that something we all crave? We crave relationship and the chance to express ourselves and be heard.

Loving and trusting God was nothing new to me, but I really began to be in complete awe of Him and the way He works. Every single day we learned something new in the morning only to see Him walk us through it in the afternoon. I had never been on any sort of missions trip before and I always wondered about the stories missionaries told upon their return. Sometimes I even wondered if they were exaggerating or if they had purposefully set up scenarios that would give them great stories to share when they got home. How is it possible that everyone who goes on a missions trip always seems to come home with at least one amazing story? It has since occurred to me that God is always with us, but when you're actually seeking Him and trying desperately to understand what you're being taught, He shows up. There's no possible way He *wouldn't* show up when you put it into practice. That's why when we sit at home in our comfortable houses with heat and air-conditioning, we're ignorant enough to make comments like, "If God's real, why do such awful things happen in the world?" Those who actually follow

God to places where awful things have happened come back even stronger in their faith. It's easy to judge Him when you're nowhere near Him. Much like it's easy to judge the person you know nothing about.

I have many more Remix stories, but I'll share just one more. Near the end of the week, we learned about contact, or touch, and the importance of it. In the morning, we heard a story about an orphanage in China where hundreds upon hundreds of children went to die. The children didn't die because they weren't being cared for or fed, but because there were so many of them and so few workers. The workers simply didn't have time to pick up these children and hold them. This complete lack of contact literally left them to wither away until they finally died.

That afternoon, we took the teens to a home in Toronto that housed people with all sorts of mental and physical disorders. As we walked in the front door, we heard a man with Tourette Syndrome screaming out profanities. I was concerned about bringing the teens inside as they looked terrified. I didn't want to put them in a situation they weren't equipped to handle.

Thankfully, I wasn't the one leading this group. It turns out I hadn't given these teens nearly enough credit. We spent an hour or two doing odd jobs to help the staff. We folded laundry and cleaned out a locker room and washroom. We gathered trash and took it out to the garbage bins, etc. When we were finished, they asked if we would spend some time with the residents before heading out, as they didn't get many guests.

The teens were nervous but quickly found things to do. A couple of them began to play pool with some of the residents. One young man went to the piano. While he played, some of the residents swayed and clapped. A few of the girls entertained the older women by dancing to the music. I looked around the room at how all these teens who had entered the building nervously now chatted and laughed with the people who lived there. I was so incredibly proud of all of them. It appeared as though everyone had been paired up and there was nobody for me to visit with, so I stood quietly against the back wall and prayed for everyone.

It was then that I noticed an older woman sitting alone in her wheelchair. She was hunched over so far that I barely realized there was anyone in the wheelchair at all. I decided to visit with her. I knelt down and introduced myself. There was no response; she stared straight down at her lap. I asked what her name was and, again, no response. I saw that she didn't appear to have the ability to talk and I wasn't sure what to do or say. I felt uncomfortable squatting beside her, so I spotted a chair and pulled it up next to her. I thought about what we had learned earlier that day about contact. I was nervous because we live in a world that teaches us to be very mindful of our personal space and I certainly didn't want to overstep my boundaries with this complete stranger.

I thought to myself that I would make an attempt to connect with her out of godly love, and if she began to scream or get upset I would quickly back away and apologize. I slowly reached out my hand and placed it over top of hers. For the first time, she made an attempt to look up at me. She had the biggest, bluest eyes and they rolled all over the place, as though she couldn't focus. It brought me back to Clarence's last days when he was on so much pain medication that he couldn't focus. There was something comforting in feeling as though I had seen those eyes before.

I spoke to her quietly. "I'm not sure if you can understand me, but I just want to tell you that we're here today to let you know that God loves you very much. You have not been forgotten. You have not been abandoned. You are not alone in this place."

As I spoke these words, she very slowly began to stroke my hand with her thumb. The more I told her how much God loved her, the more she lowered her head. By the time I had spoken these few sentences, her head was bowed so low it was nearly touching her knees. I believe she heard these words and knew they were true. I believe that she was in desperate need of loving contact and that the reminder of God's love was so amazing and humbling that all she could do was bow her head.

We were then told that we had to leave. Before getting up, I told her to never forget that He would be with her always. She stroked my hand one last time. I patted hers and we were off.

I just made it outside when the tears began to flow. I pray that God impacted her life that day as much as He did mine. We tend to say things like, "She's in such a bad state, it would probably be better if she just passed away." What we're too ignorant to realize is that sometimes God needs us to live longer than we may even want. Sometimes it takes that long to reach us. Maybe she had never heard from God before in such a powerful way and it took a failing body and mind to bring her to that place where she would run into a young woman who just so happened to be chasing after Jesus and trying desperately to follow His lead. Or maybe He needed her to be there for me. Maybe that was strictly for my own benefit. I don't know. What I do know is that we have a crazy way of loving or hating God based upon whether He allows someone to live long enough or too long. We judge Him because we think we know when it's someone's time to go.

I've come to learn that God wants our hearts and souls. These are more important things to Him than whether or not we get eighty healthy years of life on earth. I believe that Clarence's death was very impactful to a lot of people, causing them to start thinking more seriously about life and death. As a result, they wondered about this God of the Bible. If even one person came to know Christ as a result of his death, that far outweighs the fact that he died at such a young age. I realize that now and trust my life, and the lives of those around me, to Him completely. Obviously, I would love to grow old with Greg and live many healthy, happy years together, but should God need to call one of us home early to speak into the life of another who isn't quite there yet, I will accept that, too.

All I know is that I made Him a promise a long time ago and I intend to keep it. When my time comes, with my very last breath I intend to praise God and ask Jesus to lead the way, because where He goes, I will follow. My only hope is that I at least share my last moments with one other person so that he or she may have the opportunity to be impacted. That way, even my death can be used to serve His good purposes.

When Faith Meets Preparation

I came home from Remix feeling challenged, excited, and having a renewed energy and desire to serve God.

September rolled around and Sunday school started up again at church. Ryan Young, the youth pastor, asked me if I would consider starting a weekly small group Bible study for teen girls. I was nervous about this because, while God had shown me that I could lead when He put me in situations to do so, this felt as though it came out of nowhere. I wasn't sure it was God's intent for me to do this. I said I would pray about it. I did, and I also took it to my small group to ask their opinions, primarily those of Pat and Mike. I knew them to be godly people who were prayerful in their own lives, and when giving advice to others. They both reminded me that I'd already been leading in some ways. They felt that Ryan wouldn't have asked if he didn't think I was capable. They suggested I do it and stop fretting.

Ryan and I then sent out invitations stating when and where the girls would meet. For three weeks I showed up and waited, and for three weeks nobody came. I didn't have a great plan as to what we would study, but I had just read a wonderful book called *A Lineage of Grace*, by Francine Rivers, which caused me to look at the women in the Bible differently—and at women in general. I thought it might be nice to read the stories of five biblical women—Tamar,

Rahab, Ruth, Bathsheba, and Mary—to see how our stories relate to theirs.

While I could have been frustrated by the fact that not a single person showed up, I actually felt blessed for the experience. For those three nights, I was able to sit alone in the church and have some great quiet time with God. I wondered if maybe He had prompted me to do this because He knew I would be in need of this time with Him. That may sound crazy, but God really is amazing like that. You just never know how He'll work things out in your life. The teen girls' small group idea was scrapped. This may have been the wrong time for it.

Within a year, a few things changed in my life. Mike, who led the small group I was a member of, decided he needed a much-deserved break. At first it seemed nice to have my Wednesday nights free, but within a few short weeks I began to greatly miss those weekly meetings. As a result, I decided to do my own personal Bible study. I began to read the Bible, but this time more slowly. I took notes and wrote down my thoughts and feelings. Then my friend Melissa, who also missed these meetings, contacted me and suggested we might continue to meet. We got together and I shared with her some of the exciting things I had learned as a result of my personal study. We had a great talk about what God was doing in our lives.

We later decided that as much as we enjoyed visiting, it was the God-centred part of our visit that we appreciated most. Since there was no other small group for us, maybe it was time to start our own. We thought of a few girls we believed would get along well and complement each other. I sent out an email to each proposing our idea. In a few short weeks, our ladies' Bible study began.

I prayed a great deal leading up to the first get-together and felt as though we desperately needed some ground rules so this didn't just become a regular night to visit where God was left out. I welcomed everyone to my home and we agreed to take turns hosting. We also agreed that we would arrive with our own beverages and no food was to be served. We wouldn't do anything that would cause people to feel as though they had to compete with the other hostesses. These visits were to be God-centred.

I explained some of the things God had been walking me through, and that the last thing I wanted was to be part of a small group that always told me I was doing things right. I wanted to belong to a group that challenged me and kept me accountable. I wanted to move forward in faith. That meant that if I was struggling in a particular area, I could confide in these women. I didn't want them to make excuses for me or try to make me feel better. What I wanted was for them to lift me up to God in prayer and speak truth into my life, even if it hurt to hear the truth.

I had a difficult time praying out loud in front of others. I would literally burst into tears if put on the spot and asked to pray in public. Greg was the only reason I got past that. When we first started dating, I explained that I couldn't pray in front of others, so he would always pray on our behalf before dinner.

One night he said to me, "Jen, do you appreciate your job?

"Of course I do!"

"Do you appreciate that you have food to eat?"

Again, of course I did.

"So say that, out loud," he replied. "God does a lot for us. The least we can do is acknowledge these things."

I saw Greg's point and that night my prayer over dinner was, "Thank you so much for great jobs, food on the table, and for bringing Greg into my life. Amen."

Greg smiled. "Well done."

He then insisted on a semi-regular basis that I be the one to pray over our meals. After a while it didn't feel weird or awkward. Once you can pray in front of one other person, there isn't much difference when doing it in front of five or ten.

I explained what Greg had done for me to these girls who would soon become fast friends, and asked that we start to do this for each other. I knew that some of the others weren't too keen on praying out loud either, so I told them we were going to start our Bible study with a series by Mark Driscoll out of Mars Hill Church called "Pray Like Jesus." This was a five-part video series. I agreed not to single anyone out or ask them to pray out loud, as I didn't want them to feel nervous or worried, but by the end of five weeks of learning to pray like Jesus, if we weren't all comfortable enough praying out loud, then maybe we needed to stop and re-evaluate where we were in our faith and why our walk had stopped in this one spot.

They all agreed and we began watching the videos. We grew to be excited over what we learned and how quickly we felt connected to one another. Satan is frustrated by one solid Christian who knows and loves God, but when a group gets together and becomes even stronger in faith, this threatens everything he strives to accomplish. Needless to say, it wasn't more than a week or two before our group was under attack from all directions.

People were soon missing nights for one reason or another, personal insults were hurled at us from one of the members, and in less than three weeks we were on the verge of folding. I was very much in favour of it coming to an end. The hurt and frustration was unreal. I began to pray about it and God singlehandedly walked me through what to say and do with each girl. He had me email one girl who I was happy to never speak with again. He also had me send encouraging messages to others. He had me make personal visits, and even babysit on occasion. God stitched this group back together more tightly than it had been when we first started.

We're now a tight group of five women and I would do anything for any of these girls. I can honestly say that I love them as individuals and a group. Depending on the day and our moods, I may get annoyed, but that's nothing more than life getting in the way. I trust them with everything and have been loved and supported through so much. If I were frustrated in my marriage, these are the kind of women who would allow me to vent, but they'd never talk badly about Greg. They know that he's amazing to me, and if I ever get tripped up and forget that, these women will be there to remind me of it. They don't exist in my life to tell me that I'm right, but rather to help me refocus on God until I get right.

They pray not only for me, but for my entire family. They accompany me when I go to Kingston to visit Tom in jail. They know that my faith is strong but I am weak, and they're faithful to forgive me when my weakness causes me to stumble. I thank God every day for these godly women. I pray for them always. I pray they know just how much they mean to me, and just in case they aren't sure, I need to state this very specifically: Bethany, Cara, Melissa, and Tara, you ladies are a blessing in my life and I thank you from the bottom of my heart for being there for me, and more importantly, for not leaving. I know that there are "seasons" for relationships, and people may come and go in our lives, but for the first time I believe God has surrounded me with women who won't leave me. Time or distance may separate us, but our love and prayers will keep us connected. I thank you all.

By the time we finished the "Pray Like Jesus" series, I felt we had each experienced incredible change and blessings in our lives. We began to pray out loud for each other and each other's families. We often paused in our study to pray about something that had come up in conversation so that we wouldn't forget or get distracted and later forget. We began to contact each other via email to simply say, "Hope you're having a good day, I'm praying for you today."

These may seem like small things, but when you're having a bad day at work and somebody emails you just to let you know they're thinking of you and praying for you, it feels like a big thing. We're all moving forward in faith, and as a result the group flourished.

To Be Redeemed

The second video series we decided to watch was called "Redeeming Ruth." This, too, was an amazing series. Each video was interesting, funny, and truthful! Not a week went by that we weren't able to see our own lives and situations played out in this story.

Ruth is the story of a woman who finds herself widowed after ten years of marriage. Both her father-in-law and brother-in-law passed away at roughly the same time. Ruth, her mother-in-law Naomi, and her sister-in-law Orpah, find themselves without husbands, sons, or fathers. Naomi decides to move back to Bethlehem, where her people are from and where God is worshipped. Ruth and Orpah decide to join Naomi. Along the way, Naomi tells them to turn back. She has no men in her life to offer them as husbands and no way to take care of them. She tells them to return to their parents' homes and find other men to marry. Orpah decides to do this and turns back. Ruth, though, has had a genuine heart conversion and she has come to believe in the God of the Bible. She says she wants to follow God as well, so she won't turn back. Naomi and Ruth continue on to Bethlehem.

Ruth asks for Naomi's blessing and trusts God that He will provide for them and guide her. With that, she heads out to glean wheat in farmers' fields. It would ordinarily be dangerous for a young woman to walk alone down farm roads, especially an outsider like herself. She has faith, though, and it just so happens that she ends up finding work in Boaz's field. Boaz is an incredibly godly man who treats others with kindness and love, takes his responsibilities seriously, is wise with his finances, prays for others often, and oh yeah, he just so happens to be single.

Mark Driscoll explains in this video series how as women, we should want to be like Ruth. We want to be godly and faithful, bold in following the Lord, mature in accepting advice from older, wiser women, and patient in waiting for God to provide in all areas of our lives. He also explains how men should strive to be like Boaz and what it looks like when you find a "Boaz." Boaz is good and godly. He is responsible and mature. He takes care of his business and the people in his life. He is honourable and well-respected. Boaz is a redeemer.

In the end, he redeems Ruth. He takes this woman, who has worshipped other gods, been married, widowed, poor, and struggled to find food and shelter, and he redeems her. Boaz marries Ruth and they end up having a child together. This child was named Obed. Obed grew up to have a son named Jesse, who would have a son named David—as in King David.

Driscoll explains how this is probably the greatest love story of all time and then proceeds to show how it parallels the story of Jesus. Jesus loves us, sees the potential in us, and ultimately saves us from the desperate lives we end up leading when left to our own devices.

As I watched this series, I couldn't help but think about my first real boyfriend and how I tried to make that relationship work at all costs, just because I had been impatient. I hadn't wanted to admit that it had been a bad decision on my part. Suffering through a bad relationship somehow seemed better than admitting defeat.

I thought that maybe, just maybe, had I heard this message and in this way, I may have made some better choices for myself. With each video, this feeling became stronger and by the end of the six weeks I felt as though it might be worth asking Ryan at our church if he would support my running a six-week small group for teen girls. This time, the timing felt right and I had content worth sharing. Excited about the idea, I was sure Ryan would say yes.

Before I even had a chance to ask Ryan, I had a crazy dream. Unlike other dreams, I woke up from this one crying hysterically and remembering every single detail. It was an intense dream in which I happened to walk in on a little girl (maybe two years old) being badly abused. I ended up taking her out of the situation and straight to a hospital to receive medical treatment. As we sat in the waiting room, she leaned heavily against me, staring down at the floor and looking completely broken. I looked around at the other children in the waiting room and noticed how they all played with toys or read books with parents. I looked back down at this girl and something happened that I'm completely embarrassed to admit: I began to see my own life and how it had just been changed as a result of what I'd witnessed. I realized that things were never going to be the same for me, and this frightened me. One day I knew exactly where my life was heading, and the next day it was all up in the air and I had no clue what was going on or what to expect. I blamed this innocent little girl and pushed her away with my foot. "Sit up straight," I hissed at her. "Why can't you play with toys and act normal like the other girls and boys?"

This poor little girl curled up into an even tighter ball, careful not to touch me. In that moment, I heard a voice say, *"This is your girl."* I looked at her again, but this time I looked at her as though she were my own. My heart broke into tiny pieces. Not only had she been badly damaged by someone else, but even I, who was trying to help her, had somehow gotten caught up in my own thoughts and fears and damaged her further.

I leaned over and whispered in her ear, "I'm so sorry. You didn't deserve that. You don't have to be like the other boys or girls at all. You're perfect just the way you are, you know that?"

Like a puppy who has been kicked but runs right back to his owner wanting to love and be loved, the girl turned her big blue eyes up to mine and smiled brightly. She babbled happily and I scooped her up. She talked and talked. I couldn't make out a word she said, but I smiled and nodded anyway. The more I loved and encouraged her, the more she came out of her shell. She and I ended up going to therapy and healing together.

I decided that I wanted to adopt her, but I had no idea how. Who was she? I didn't know who her parents were or where she had come from. Papers were filed with the courts and, when nobody claimed her, she was quickly mine. I watched as this little girl who had almost been destroyed grew into an incredible young lady.

Everywhere we went, she turned heads. She was beautiful and bubbly and people were drawn to her immediately. She lit a room up just by walking into it and I realized that there was a time when I would have been jealous of all the attention she got, but at this point in my life nothing could be further from the truth. I loved watching her interact with others and see the way everyone who met her loved her. The more attention she got, the happier and more excited I became.

Then, one day, we were walking through a grocery store when a lady walked up and said, "Aren't you a pretty little girl?" The woman reached out to brush her cheek. I had a flashback of seeing her being abused and lunged at this woman, prepared to do serious damage to her.

Just before I got to her, the girl said to me, "It's okay, Mommy. She's a good person. I can tell."

I stopped and stared. Had she just called me Mommy? I apologized to the woman and scooped her up. Groceries no longer mattered. We walked down the road to a park and I watched my little girl play on the swings—my daughter.

Then I woke up. I cried over the damage that had been done to such a sweet girl. I cried shameful tears over my own part in hurting her. I cried tears of joy at seeing her come out the other side and end up being a blessing to anyone who knew her. I just cried.

I had no idea what this dream meant. I rarely dream, and when I do I normally forget the details almost immediately. This dream was different. I lay in bed wondering what it meant. Were Greg and I about to get pregnant? Were we supposed to adopt? Was I about to encounter a girl who had been abused? Why had I lashed out at her in such an awful way? Was I a despicable person? Was God showing me my nature and that he was about to walk me through it?

I began to pray, asking the Holy Spirit to guide my prayers. I didn't even know where to begin. I prayed, and by the end I had learned a few things. There are a lot of hurting women in the world. We haven't all been abused, but we've all suffered hurt in one way or another. I felt compelled to show the Ruth videos to the teen girls. I also felt as though I was on the right track, but that I needed to think bigger. Finally, I physically felt as though a blanket was being lovingly wrapped around me and I was told that I had just been given a heart for women.

I got up and got ready for work, then spent the better part of the day trying to make sense of all this.

I went out for dinner with Bethany and showed her the dream, which by now I had typed out. Once she read it, I explained what had happened, telling her that I felt as though I needed to think bigger. I told her about my idea to show the Ruth videos to the teen girls in her youth group. She knew they would really appreciate the series and offered to sell them on it. I intended to ask Dave Lane, a youth pastor I knew from my former church, if his teens would join as well. I knew he would support me once I told him what it was all about.

Now that I had a larger group in mind, I needed to find a venue to hold it in. Originally, I would have just met with the three or four teen girls from our church in a small room at the church. Now that it was growing, we needed a better location, something neutral. I feared that if we hosted the event at one church, girls from the other churches wouldn't feel as confident about attending. I got stuck at this point, and then life got busy.

Greg and I had places to go and people to see. Work became busy and, to be honest, the whole "Redeeming Ruth" series dropped off my radar. Then, at small group one evening, we each prayed before calling it a night. Melissa started to pray about this event (by now everyone in our small group was aware of my plans), praying that God would find the perfect venue for me. I thought this was interesting since I hadn't mentioned that I was struggling over the venue. Again, we really underestimate the power of prayer.

Shortly after that, I woke up one Saturday morning with a singular thought: The Sarnia Lambton 9 Famous Players Movie Theatre. The location was great, the seating would be more than enough (not to mention comfortable), buses ran to and from it, and the mall was nearby so moms could drop off their daughters, kill some time walking around if they wanted, and return to pick them up. Perfect!

This was quickly replaced with other thoughts: *Are you crazy? What if only five girls show up? What do you need an entire movie theatre for? How much will it cost? How do I even go about doing it?* This quickly stopped me from getting too excited. Before I completely gave up on the idea, though, I thought to myself, *Wait a minute. This wasn't my own idea. I'm not that creative. I never would have thought of something like this. If this is in fact from God, what's the harm in trying?*

I had some running around to do in Sarnia that day and decided to stop by the theatre on my way home and ask to speak with a manager. I went to Sarnia and ran my errands, then promptly chickened out and returned home.

The next morning, Greg and I went to church. At the end of the sermon, the pastor tacked on an extra little bit that didn't seem to go with the sermon. He started to talk about blind faith.

"What if a family struggles to pay the bills and put food on the table, but they really want to tithe and give ten percent to the church as a symbol of their love and trust of God?" he asked. "Maybe the mom or dad could take a second job and work more hours, scrimping and saving until finally they could afford the bills *and* give to God. Well, that's not blind faith. That's relying on yourself to take care of the issues and then giving God what you have left. If, however, that same family decided to give their *first* ten percent to the church, knowing full well that they would then be short and unable to cover the cost of the bills and food… *that* is blind faith." He paused before going on. "There's someone in this room right now who's struggling with this. You're wondering how you can manage things on your own rather than having blind faith and allowing God to work out the details."

He encouraged us to let go of control and follow blindly. He said he would be excited to hear the stories that came from his congregation once people started to do this.

My heart pounded and I knew he was speaking directly into my life. I went home and told Greg everything. I explained about my initial desire to run a six-week small group, my dream, the sermon, and that I felt I was supposed to try to get a movie theatre to host the event.

This is the part in my story where I thank God for providing me with such an amazing, godly husband. I love Greg and value his opinion. At any point in time, he could have shut this down. A simple "I don't think you really need to rent a movie theatre for something like this, do you?" or "That could cost a lot, I don't know if this is the best way to spend our money" and I would have caved. Instead, he recognized the ways I was being led and decided that he didn't want to get in the way of God's plans. He didn't make fun of me or laugh at my ideas. He didn't tell me I was crazy or make me feel as though I was. What Greg said was, "That's pretty cool, Jen. I don't see the harm in asking about it. The worst they'll do is say no. And if they do that, then you'll know that you misunderstood and I'm sure He'll lead you in the right direction from there."

With God's prompting and my husband's blessing, I decided to follow.

The next day, I looked up the theatre's website and found the contact information. I sent an email describing what I wanted to do, asking if it was possible. I got no reply.

A few days later, I received an email apologizing for the delayed response and stating that, yes, I could book a theatre to show a video. The minimum time to book the theatre was two hours and it would cost five hundred dollars an hour. That was a thousand dollars for each of the six nights—six thousand dollars! The email went on to say that because this was a non-profit event, they would give me a discount of fifty percent. This was a great discount, but still… three thousand dollars was a lot of money. I barely noticed the amount, though. I was amazed that God had led me here and that it was actually becoming a possibility! I told Greg right away and he shared my excitement. I think we both knew at this point that God had something amazing planned and it was far bigger than what we were seeing. Both Greg and I were about to get a bonus from work. I thought that mine would be four percent at most. I was perfectly happy with this since I never expected a bonus and considered it just that—a bonus. I met with my boss that week to find out that the company had had a great year and so I was actually going to receive a 12.25% bonus. This would more than cover the cost of the theatre.

God, You are amazing!

It was settled. I rented the movie theatre for one night a week for six weeks. I stood up in front of our church and explained everything that had happened and asked that they support me in prayer. The whole church was abuzz! People were looking forward to convincing their daughters and friends to attend. There was a general feeling that God wanted this to be big for a reason and someone was going to be very changed by this series.

The catch was that the following week I was going on vacation for eight days in Costa Rica with Greg and two other couples, only to return in the early hours of Saturday morning. The series was going to start that Monday. I felt frantic about not having enough time to prepare.

The first thing I stressed over was what to call the event. I wrote down a list of possible names, but none of them were quite right. Then Bethany called to see how I was doing and I explained that I was stuck without a name. Without a name, I wouldn't be able to print flyers or have people spread the word. This felt important and it needed to be good. She asked me why I was really doing this. What was the purpose?

"I don't know," I said. "I guess I want girls to see these videos and really understand the way God loves them. I want them to see themselves the way God does and, as a result, love what they see."

And there I had it. "Love at First Sight: See yourself for the first time and love what you see!" This would be the title and tagline. I printed off simple flyers indicating the time, dates, and location and planned to stick them up wherever I could. I contacted the local radio station and they agreed to announce it on the air at least once before it began. I contacted someone at the local paper, who agreed to write an article about it. Bethany created a Facebook group called "Love at First Sight" and, as a symbol, she used a picture of an eye with a pupil in the shape of a heart.

I received an email from Ryan Young stating that he had felt led to create a poster for me, but I wasn't to feel pressured to use it. I could hardly believe my eyes when I saw it. It was truly beautiful—a picture of a young girl with stunning green eyes and, if you looked closely, you could see that her pupil was the shape of a heart. I asked Ryan if he had seen Bethany's Facebook group and he said he hadn't realized a group had been created. I felt as though their use of the same visual reinforced that our title was good. Everything was coming together as it should.

A teen from church, Breanne, spent a Sunday afternoon driving around Sarnia with me, putting up posters at every bus stop. We tried to put them in stores, but few would actually allow it. Breanne told me to leave a bunch with her and she would put them up around the high school, even giving some to her friends who attended different schools. That would help get the word out.

Two days later, I was in Sarnia again and decided to drive by some of the bus stops to see how the posters looked. They had all been removed. I made my rounds, posting them one more time. I left for Costa Rica feeling as though I had done everything I could, that this vacation would be a good chance for me to rest and pray in preparation for the weeks to come. I decided not to worry at all about whether or not the word got out back home, because I had faith that God would take care of the details. We had a fantastic vacation with really incredible friends.

When we returned home, it was go-time.

I went to church Sunday morning. When I saw Breanne, I asked if she had put the posters up around her school. She said she hadn't and my heart sank. It wasn't for lack of trying, though. Because this wasn't a school-sanctioned event, the school wouldn't let Breanne advertise it. My heart sank even lower knowing that this would be the case at the other schools as well. Once Sunday school ended, Ryan asked if I was prepared. Just then, his wife joined us and said, "Oh yeah, that starts tomorrow, doesn't it? It's at the Imperial Theatre, right?"

I burst into tears. Nobody even knew it was taking place, and those who did know thought it was at a different location. I felt as though I had failed in a mighty way. God had given me one thing to do and I'd missed it. I choked this out between sobs and Ryan assured me that I was wrong. He told me that he himself had been running into people and telling them about the event and they had seemed excited about it. He had met at least a couple of people who had agreed to let him post signs in their storefronts. He was confident that the person or persons who God wanted to attend would absolutely get the invitation. He prayed for me and the tension left my body immediately.

This was going to be okay. This wasn't *my* event, but God's. I had been clearly led to do this and God doesn't lead us to do big things just to have nobody show up. I reminded myself that if even one person showed up, maybe that was the one I had been led to do it for. This wasn't a numbers game, but an opportunity to follow and be faithful. Whether or not I would even know the outcome was yet to be determined, but I realized that the outcome might not be for me to know.

The first night, I showed up to see "Love at First Sight" listed as one of the movies playing and my heart skipped a beat. We were really doing this! Twenty-seven people showed up all together, including myself and the girls from my small group who had already seen the series. The theatre felt incredibly empty, but the girls who showed up seemed to really like the video and all said they would invite friends the following week.

For the second week, we had thirty-six people. Then forty-eight. We then took a Monday off for Easter, and when we returned the week after we had forty-two. I thought maybe we had lost momentum, and sure enough, on the fifth week we had just thirty-two people show. I was disappointed because I knew how amazing the sixth and final video was. To my surprise, on the last and most important night, fifty-one women came.

The videos were powerful and nobody who attended left unaffected. Even me and my friends, who had seen them once before, were amazed at how many new things we picked up on.

Each week I spoke for a little bit before and after the videos. The girls were given an opportunity to chat with me or one of the other women, should they need to talk. The videos on dating really struck a nerve with most of them and they started to understand how valuable they were, that they were worthy of having great, healthy relationships, and not just the first relationship that came along.

Two different themes emerged from these Monday night get-togethers. Mark Driscoll taught us the gospel truth about Jesus, and how to take steps and make decisions much like Ruth.He showed us how to move from a low point in life to the ultimate point in life. It was my job, on the other hand, to get the girls to see themselves the way God saw them right then, before they even took another step. It was my job to show them that they were perfectly created, completely loved, fully forgiven, and of incredible worth. It was my job to instill in them the confidence to know that they, too, could walk in faith, as Ruth had done.

I was amazed at how God gave me the exact words to say each night. These videos were changing young girls' lives right before my eyes. I received a lot of positive feedback and continue to hear great things. Mostly, though, I know that where God leads, I will follow.

I'm amazed that I still hesitate at times, but I pray this goes away in time. I would like to see my faith so strong that when God says jump, I leap without even looking. I feel as though that day isn't too far off, and I'm excited to get there. I still pray that He'll stay with me and be patient, because I know I'm not there yet.

Hearts Healed and Love Lived Out

It's important to note that my mom drove every week to support me in the "Love at First Sight" series. We have made huge strides in our relationship. I don't say that our relationship wasn't very good for a long time to embarrass her, but to point out that our story is a great one, one that may be used to encourage others.

Mothers and daughters have such high expectations of each other. From the time we're born, our mothers carry us, nurture us, and develop high hopes for us. Sometimes the bar seems as though it has been set too high and we're set up to fail. On the other hand, as daughters we tend to believe that if anyone should know and understand us, it should be our mothers. That's a lot of pressure to place on our moms.

My mom and I went through years of misunderstanding each other, and ultimately hurting each other's feelings. I don't think it was ever an issue of not loving one another, but sometimes hurt feels as though it trumps love. We would rather focus on the hurt and walk away than focus on love and draw near. That's what my mom and I did to each other.

Only when I prayed for God to reveal myself to me did He really begin to work on this relationship. I believe He waited until this time in my life because I was finally ready to hear it. What He revealed to me was that, yes, my mom had said and done hurtful things to me. But I had never forgiven her. I had never turned the other cheek. I had set such high expectations for her that the minute she messed up, I clung to that and fired back at her the first chance I got. It occurred to me that if two people beat each other up to the point where they were no longer even recognizable, did it really matter who threw the first punch? The answer is no. I was so busy feeling justified in my hurt that it never occurred to me that I had been doing and saying hurtful things of my own. For so many years, all I had wanted was an apology. What God showed me is that I owed my mom an apology.

This was an incredibly humbling time for me. It took a couple of weeks to work myself up to the point where I felt I could apologize. I really felt that I owed her an apology in person, but as hard as I tried, I just couldn't seem to force myself to get there. Finally I decided that an apology over the phone was better than no apology at all. I called her and we had a nice talk… and then I finally did it. I apologized. I told her that I knew I had said and done so many hurtful things over the years and that I had never stopped to acknowledge what I had done, or to ask for forgiveness. I asked if she could forgive me for all I had done and she said she didn't know what I was talking about, but yes. She *did* know what I was talking about, though, and I have a feeling that apology must have felt pretty good considering it was such a long time coming.

We have been better about calling each other since then, and seeing her drive nearly an hour each week to support me in something that was so close to my heart had a healing effect on my life. Who knows? Maybe God had me rent an entire theatre just so that my mom and I could watch those videos and start over. At any rate, I'm grateful for new beginnings.

Greg and I will be married two years this July 3, 2011. We still marvel at the fact that we actually made it to the altar. I was tricked so many times into believing he didn't love me when the truth is, nobody could have exercised as much patience and understanding as Greg did. He took being a godly boyfriend to a new level. I love looking back at all the times I blamed him for things out of his control and wanted to break up with him, just to have God tell me, "No."

I also love a certain story Greg tells. Once, when we were arguing, I started to cry, as per usual, blaming him for everything that was wrong in my life. He had reached his breaking point with me and he opened his mouth to say, "Look, I'm sorry, Jen, but this just isn't working. I wish you well, but I can't do this anymore."

Just as he was about to say the words, this came out: "I'm *sorry!*" He says he swears he didn't know how "I'm sorry" came out when that was the last thing he intended to say. Secretly, though, we both know how it happened.

I said it at our wedding, and I'll say it again: Satan may have tripped me up more than a few times, but that isn't such a big deal. For one to cause another to stumble and fall, that isn't so difficult. For one to cause two, who are holding hands and running in the same direction, to fall—*that* is difficult." That's what God saw in us. We were two individuals doing our best to chase after Jesus and God brought us together, knowing that two people who are bound together with God in the centre are a force to be reckoned with. Satan may have succeeded in toying with us in our dating lives, but God had plans to see us married. Even our own desires wouldn't stand in the way of His plans for us. It is by the grace of God that we're together, and that we're so incredibly happy.

I cannot imagine my life without Greg in it. He didn't get what was left of me. I feel as though Clarence took my heart with him when he left. God gave me a new heart with new desires that exists wholly to love my Father in Heaven and my husband on earth. No regrets, no "what ifs," no "if I could turn back time"—just excitement at the ability to live in the here and now, knowing that God knows the plans He has for me, plans to prosper and not to harm me. Plans to give me hope and a future.

Afterword:
If My Life Hasn't Ended,
How Can the Story?

I recently attended Temple Baptist Church in Sarnia every evening for a week. An outside group of pastors came in to lead a "revival series." The sermons were amazing and it was a great week of being uplifted and encouraged. I was reminded to never give up.

Of all the things that were said, though, my favourite came from Pastor Steven Jones, the senior pastor at Temple Baptist. Just before leading us in prayer one evening, he spoke of Exodus 33:15, which says, *"Then Moses said to him, 'If your Presence does not go with us, do not send us up from here.'"* Moses didn't want to take another step if the Lord God wasn't with him and his people.

"How do you know if you're under God's judgement?" Pastor Steve then asked. "These were God's chosen people and He took care of them by providing food, cloud cover by day, and a pillar of fire to lead them by night. He was clearly with them and blessing them, yet they were under His judgement. So, how do you know if you're under God's judgement? It takes you forty years to make what should have been a two-week journey, that's how you know. The scenery never changes. You walk by the same rocks, and maybe even the same beautiful oasis, but everything stays the same."

I found that to be one of the most profound things I'd heard in a long time.

I was wondering how to end this story of mine because it is my life, and life keeps on going. Well, I know that it's my heart's desire to never stop moving. My hope is that by the time you read this and ask, "What's new?" I will have all sorts of new crazy stories to share, because I'm still chasing after Jesus. When you do that, He never leads you in circles. He takes your life, which you may have once thought to be small and meaningless, and fills it with joy and purpose. He takes you on a journey that never ends, never repeats itself, and never ceases to challenge and stretch you in every possible way.

This book has come to an end, but my story, much like Ruth's, is a story of love, redemption, hope, and God.